THE
TEA
COMPANION

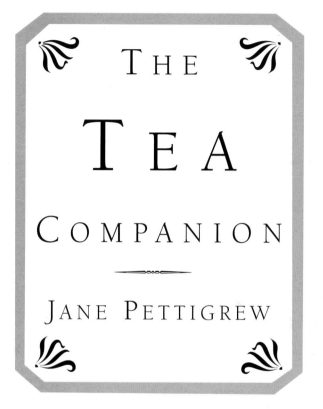

THE
TEA
COMPANION

JANE PETTIGREW

MACMILLAN • USA

Library of Congress Cataloging-in-Publication Data

Pettigrew, Jane.
The tea companion / Jane Pettigrew.
    p.   cm.
Includes index.
ISBN 0-02-861727-4
1. Tea. 2. Tea–Guidebooks. 3. Tea–History. I. Title.
TX817.T3P48   1997
641.3'372–dc21   97-5770
                                                          CIP

This book was designed and produced by
Quintet Publishing Limited
6 Blundell Street
London N7 9BH

Creative Director: Richard Dewing
Art Director: Clare Reynolds
Designer: Dave Goodman
Project Editor: Clare Hubbard
Editor: Rosie Hankin
Photographer: Paul Forrester
Map Illustrations: Richard Chasemore

Typeset in Great Britain by
Central Southern Typesetters, Eastbourne
Manufactured in Singapore by Universal Pte Ltd.
Printed in China by Leefung-Asco Printers Ltd.

AUTHOR'S ACKNOWLEDGMENTS
As is always the case with the international tea industry, a wide variety of people
all around the world have been extremely generous with advice and help in the preparation
of this book. I would like to express my sincere thanks to everyone who has sent tea samples,
tewares, information, and photographs. I must say a special 'thank you' to five people
in particular Kitticha Sangmanée of Mariage Frères, France; Devan Shah of India Tea Importers, U.S.A.,
Mike Bunston and Dominic Beddard of Wilson Smithett UK, and Iltyd Lewis of the UK Tea Council.
Their constant generosity and guidance have been very much appreciated.
Thanks also go to Clare Hubbard at Quintet Publishing Ltd.

CONTENTS

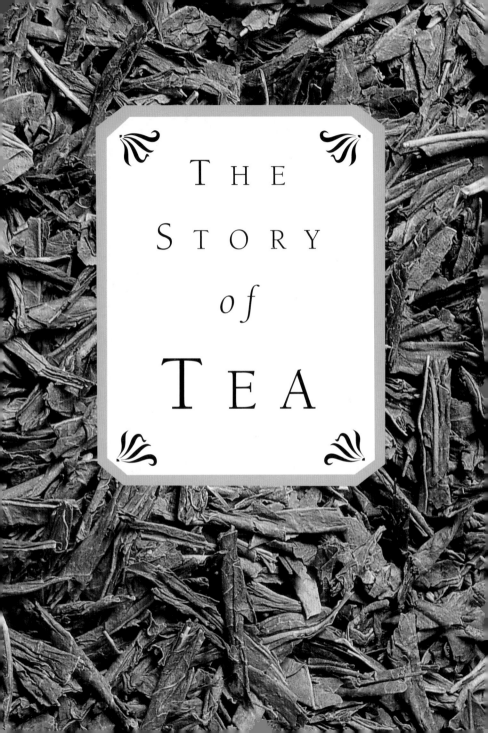

THE
STORY
of
TEA

THE HISTORY OF TEA

CHINESE ORIGINS

More tea is drunk around the world than any other beverage, and behind this everyday brew, beyond the caddies on the tea-store shelves, lies a colorful and fascinating story that weaves its way through the social and cultural history of many nations.

According to Chinese legend, this intriguing story has its origins in the discovery of tea's beneficial qualities by the Emperor Shen Nung—a scholar and herbalist who, for the sake of hygiene, drank only boiled water. It is said that one day, in the year 2737 B.C., when Shen Nung was resting under a wild tea tree, a slight breeze stirred the branches and caused a few leaves to drift gently down into the simmering water that he was preparing. He found the resulting brew deliciously refreshing and revitalizing, and so, tea was "discovered."

It is of course, impossible to know if Shen Nung really existed or whether he is simply the mythical embodiment of the agricultural, herbal, and cultural developments of ancient China. Certainly, China was not unified as an empire until the third century B.C. and it is therefore somewhat unlikely that an emperor existed as far back as 2737 B.C. But,

Shen Nung resting under a tea tree.

whatever the origins of the beverage, it is an accepted fact among scholars that tea was indeed popular in China all those years ago.

There is, however, no written reference to the leaf until the third century B.C., when a famous Chinese surgeon recommended it for increasing concentration and alertness, and an army general wrote to a nephew asking him to send some "real tea" because he was feeling old and depressed. But even the appearance of tea's name, *tu*, in ancient records causes confusion, since the same Chinese character was used for both tea and sow thistles, the only distinction being made by a variation in pronunciation after an emperor of the Han Dynasty, some time between 206 B.C. and A.D. 220, ruled that when referring to tea, the character should be pronounced *cha*. From the eighth century A.D. onward, the tracing of tea's history became somewhat simpler when one vertical stroke of the character disappeared and tea acquired its own individual character.

Chinese character for tea.

Until the third century A.D., the beverage was prepared as a medicine or tonic with the fresh green leaves gathered from wild tea trees. To match supply to an increasing demand and guarantee a regular crop, farmers began to cultivate tea bushes on their smallholdings, and a system of drying and processing was gradually developed.

Tea's popularity throughout China grew rapidly during the fourth and fifth centuries and new hill plantations were established along the Yangtze River valley. Tea was presented as a gift to emperors, began to appear in taverns, wine stores, and noodle houses, and is recorded as having been used (in the form of compressed cakes made from steamed green leaves) in barter trade with the Turkish people in A.D. 476. Tea merchants grew rich, and potters, silver traders, and goldsmiths started to manufacture expensive, elegant tea wares that carried their own significance in terms of the wealth and status of their owners.

The colorful years of the Tang Dynasty (A.D. 618–906) are often referred to as the "golden age" of tea. Tea was no longer drunk simply as a medicinal tonic but was taken as much for pleasure as for its restorative powers. The preparation and service of the liquor developed into an elaborate ceremony, while the cultivation and processing of the leaf were tightly controlled by rigid rules as to who should pluck the crop, when and how it should be gathered, how the freshly picked leaves should be handled, and the personal hygiene and diet of the young female pluckers—garlic, onions, and strong spices were strictly forbidden in case any

Hand-rolling leaves in seventeenth century China.

odor on their fingertips should contaminate the delicate leaves.

Tea became important enough during this period for a group of merchants to commission the writer, Lu Yu (A.D. 733–804), to compile the first ever book about tea. His *Cha Chang*, known as the *Classic of Tea*, describes all possible aspects, including the plant's origins and characteristics, different varieties, the processing of the leaf and the tools needed, the brewing of the beverage, tea equipage, the qualities of water in different locations, tea's medicinal qualities, and tea-drinking traditions.

During the Tang Dynasty, the young leaves, once picked, were steamed, crushed, and then mixed to a paste with plum juice which acted as a natural glue to bind the particles firmly together. The paste was then poured into molds, compressed into cakes, and baked until dry. To brew a cup of tea, the cake was roasted in the fire until it softened enough to be crushed to a powder which was then boiled in water. In some parts of China, salt was added, giving the tea a bitter aftertaste, while the most common flavorings were sweet onions, ginger, orange peel, cloves, and peppermint—added to the water before boiling with the tea or thrown in afterward.

Later, under the Song Dynasty (A.D. 960–1279), the compressed tea cake was ground to a very fine powder and whisked into boiling water to produce a frothy liquid. After drinking the first cup, more boiling water was added to the powdered tea, whisked again, and the liquor drunk; this was repeated up to seven times using the same tea. The spicy additions of the Tang Dynasty were rejected in favor of more subtle flavorings such as the essential oils of jasmine, lotus, and chrysanthemum flowers.

Until the Ming Dynasty (A.D. 1368–1644), all tea produced in China was green tea. The compressed tea cakes of previous empires had kept well and traveled unharmed as currency for trade in far-flung places. Ming tea, however, was not formed into cakes but left as loose, steamed, and dried leaf which did not keep well but quickly lost its aroma and flavor. As foreign trade increased, and tea had to retain its qualities during journeys as far afield as Europe, the profit-conscious Chinese growers developed two new types of tea—black tea and flower-scented tea. At one time, it was believed that green tea and black tea were the products of different plants, but all types start as the green leaves from the tea bush. Ming producers discovered that they could preserve the leaves by first fermenting them in air until they turned a copper red color and then halting the natural decomposition by baking. So it was that, although Europe's first imports of tea from China were of green loose leaf tea, the fashion gradually changed as Ming tea growers adapted their methods of production to suit the market.

FROM CHINA TO JAPAN

Japanese history records that in A.D. 729, the emperor, Shomu, served tea to one hundred Buddhist monks at his palace. Since no tea was grown in Japan at that time, the processed leaves must have come from China. The first seeds for cultivation are thought to have been taken to Japan by Dengyo Daishi, a monk who spent two years, from A.D. 803 to 805, studying in China. He returned home, planted the seeds in the grounds of his monastery and, when he served tea made from his first plantings to the Emperor Saga five years later, it is said that Saga enjoyed the new beverage so much that he ordered tea cultivation to be established in five provinces near the capital.

Between the end of the ninth and the eleventh centuries, Chinese-Japanese relations deteriorated and so tea, being a Chinese commodity, fell from favor and was no longer drunk at Court. However, Japanese Buddhist monks continued to drink tea to help them stay awake and to concentrate during periods of meditation. In the early twelfth century, the situation between the two nations improved and a Japanese monk by the name of Eisai was the first to pay a visit to China. He returned with more tea seeds and with the new Chinese custom of drinking powdered green tea. He also brought back an understanding of the teachings of the Rinzai Zen Buddhist sect. The tea drinking and the Buddhist beliefs developed alongside each other and, whereas the rituals associated with tea drinking in ancient China died out, the Japanese developed them into a complicated and unique ceremony. Still today, the Japanese Tea Ceremony, *Cha-no-yu*, involves a precise pattern of behavior designed to create a quiet interlude during which the host and guests strive for spiritual refreshment and harmony with the universe. In 1906, Okakura Kakuzo wrote, in his *Book of Tea*, "Teaism is a cult founded on the adoration of the beautiful among the sordid facts of everyday existence. It inculcates purity and harmony, the mystery of mutual charity, the romanticism of the social order." The Tea Ceremony captures all the essential elements of Japanese philosophy and artistic

Takeno Jhooh, a great Japanese tea master.

Advertisement for Fujiyama tea.

beauty, and interweaves four principals— harmony (with people and nature), respect (for others), purity (of heart and mind), and tranquility. As Kakuzo wrote, "Tea is more than an idealization of the form of drinking; it is a religion of the art of life." The ceremony, which can last for up to four hours, may be performed at home, in a special room set aside for the purpose, or in a tea house.

13

TEA REACHES EUROPE

It is not clear whether it was the Dutch or the Portuguese who were responsible for bringing ashore Europe's first tea in the early seventeenth century, for both nations were by that time trading in the China Seas—the Portuguese from a base at Macao on the Chinese mainland and the Dutch from the island of Java. Trade was initially in silks, brocades, and spices, but cargos soon also included tea. The Portuguese shipped China teas to Lisbon and from there, the Dutch East India Company carried goods on to Holland, France, and the Baltic ports. The Dutch transported mainly Japanese teas from Java from around 1610 but, in 1637, the company's directors wrote to their Governor General, "As tea begins to come into use by some of the people, we expect some jars of Chinese as well as Japanese teas with each ship."

The popularity of tea among all social classes in Holland grew and Dutch companies re-exported supplies to Italy, France, Germany, and Portugal. Although the French and Germans showed an interest in tea for a short time when it first arrived in Europe, they never really took to it as an everyday drink except in the northern region of Germany known as East Friesland (where it is still extremely popular today) and among the higher classes in France. Madame de Sévigné described in one of her letters how her friend, the Marquise de la Sablière, took her tea with milk and that Racine drank tea with his breakfast every day. But, by the end of the seventeenth century, coffee had become the most popular beverage in both Germany and France, and it was only in Russia and England that the market for tea was growing.

The first tea reached Russia as a gift from the Chinese to Tsar Alexis in 1618. A trade agreement, signed in 1689, marked the beginning of regular commerce, and caravans of 200–300 camels trekked to the border at Usk Kayakhta, laden with furs that were exchanged for tea. Each camel carried four chests (about 600 pounds) of tea and so progress back to Moscow was slow—the journey from Chinese grower to Russian consumer taking about 16–18 months. Until the early eighteenth century, the smoky black tea favored by the Russians (a blend still sold today by many tea companies as Russian Caravan) was expensive and therefore a drink for aristocrats. But supplies became increasingly plentiful and, by 1796, Russians were drinking more than 6,000 camel loads of tea every year. The caravan trade continued until the completion of the Trans-Siberian Railway in 1903 which allowed Chinese teas, silks, and porcelain to be transported direct to Russia in just over a week.

BRITAIN DISCOVERS TEA

Undoubtedly, some people in Britain—royalty, aristocrats, and merchants—must have heard about, and perhaps even tasted, tea well before the first recorded date of its appearance in London in 1658. Thomas Garraway, a general merchant with a store in Exchange Alley in the City of London, was

Thomas Garraway's store in Exchange Alley.

the first to advertise the new commodity for sale by auction. His announcement in the September 23–30, 1658, edition of the weekly London newspaper, *Mercurius Politicus*, read "That Excellent, and by all Physitians approved, China Drink called by the Chineans, Tcha, by other Nations Tay, alias Tee, is sold at the Sultaness Head, a Cophee-house in Sweetings Rents by the Royal Exchange, London."

Two years later, in order, no doubt, to increase sales, Garraway wrote a lengthy advertising broadsheet entitled "An Exact Description of the Growth, Quality and Vertues of the Leaf Tee" which claimed that tea would cure almost any known ailment and "maketh the Body active and lusty . . . helpeth the Head-ache, giddiness and heaviness thereof . . . taketh away the difficulty of breathing, opening Obstructions . . . is good against Liptitude, Distillations and cleareth the Sight . . . it vanquisheth heavy Dreams, easeth the Brain and strengtheneth the Memory, it overcometh superfluous Sleep, and prevents Sleepiness in general . . . it is good for Colds, Dropsies and Scurveys and expelleth Infection."

Tea's fate in Britain took a lucky turn in 1662 when King Charles II married the Portuguese princess, Catherine of Braganza. Britain's new queen was a confirmed tea drinker long before she arrived for her wedding and she brought with her, as part of her dowry, a chest of China tea. She started serving it to her aristocratic friends at Court, word of the new beverage spread, and more and more people wished to try it for themselves. But, with prices ranging from 16 to 60 shillings (equivalent to $1.20–$4.50),

Catherine of Braganza.

Thomas Twining, founder of Tom's Coffee House.

per pound it remained, in those early days, a drink for the rich and fashionable.

Ladies enjoyed tea at home, while gentlemen often drank theirs in the coffee houses that had been an established part of city life since the 1650s. Each attracted its own particular clientele—bankers, stockbrokers, politicians, journalists, or poets. The insurance company, Lloyds, started life in Edward Lloyd's coffee house in the City of London where, for the convenience of his customers, Mr Lloyd would prepare a list of ships and their cargos sailing out of the Port of London each day. In 1706, Thomas Twining, the founder of the world-famous tea company, opened Tom's Coffee House just off Strand, outside London's old city walls. In 1717, the business expanded, was renamed The Golden Lyon, and quickly became famous for selling only loose leaf tea and for serving both men and women (ladies had been banned from coffee houses and indeed no self-respecting female would have set foot inside such masculine establishments with their smoke and alcohol, male conversation, and bawdy jokes).

The high cost of tea was due to a heavy tax imposed on various popular commodities by Charles II. Duty on tea, coffee, and chocolate was assessed at 8 pence (6¢) per gallon, and this was raised to 2 shillings (16¢) in 1670. By 1689, the cheapest tea cost 7 shillings (56¢) per pound—almost an entire week's wages for an average laborer. But there was a growing demand from both rich and poor, and this led to a healthy black market which smuggled tea in from Holland, and involved entire communities— including politicians and priests—in the clandestine storage and distribution of supplies. To make the limited quantities of the genuine article go further, and thus increase profits, the tea was often adulterated with other leaves (licorice and sloe were regularly substituted), used leaves were dried and stained with molasses or clay, and ash leaves were dried, baked, trodden on the floor, sifted, and steeped in sheeps' dung. A government act of 1725 fined smugglers and unscrupulous traders the sum of £100 ($150) and, in 1730, this was increased to £10 ($15) per pound. In 1766, imprisonment became an additional penalty. Green tea was easier to pollute than black, and so, to avoid adulterated supplies, consumers turned more and more to the

Tea being smuggled ashore in eighteenth century Britain.

black, processed teas that Ming Dynasty growers had begun to produce for their foreign markets.

During the eighteenth century, tea became Britain's most popular drink, replacing ale for breakfast and gin at any other time of day. Consumption of 66,738 pounds in 1701 increased to 4,915,472 pounds by 1781, and a huge decrease in the tax in 1784 (from 119 percent to 12½ percent) led to a massive increase, reaching a total of 15,096,840 pounds in 1791. People drank tea at home and (al fresco) in London's newly fashionable Tea Gardens. The coffee houses had closed down in the early eighteenth century (by which time they had become the haunts of the idle and disreputable), to be replaced by pleasure gardens, around the outskirts of London, where people from all walks of life and all social classes, including royalty, could take the air, drink tea, and enjoy a variety of entertainments. The most famous, at Marylebone, Ranelagh, and Vauxhall, offered evening concerts, firework displays, spectacular illuminations, horse riding, gambling, bowling greens, boat trips, ballrooms with orchestras, and flower-lined walks, as well as tea and other refreshments. However, the rapid expansion of London in the early nineteenth century, and a growing taste for more sophisticated and exciting pleasures, led to the eventual closure of all the gardens.

THE BEGINNING OF AFTERNOON TEA

Until the early nineteenth century, tea was drunk at all times of the day and particularly as a digestif after the main evening meal. There was no formalized "afternoon tea" as we know it today. The credit for the invention of this truly British institution is given to Anna, the seventh Duchess of Bedford who, because of the long gap between a light luncheon and a late evening meal, is said to have experienced what she called "a sinking feeling" in the middle of the afternoon. To satisfy her pangs of hunger, she asked her maid to bring a pot of tea and a little light refreshment to her room, and she found this arrangement so agreeable that she quickly started asking her friends to join her for afternoon tea. Very soon, all of fashionable London was indulging in these gatherings to drink tea, eat dainty sandwiches and delicate cakes, and exchange gossip and general conversation. As the fashion caught on, so silversmiths, porcelain companies, and linen manufacturers began to produce all the equipage necessary for elegant teas. Cookbooks began to include instructions on how to brew and serve tea, how to organize tea receptions, which foods to serve, and how to create tea parties for all occasions. An elegant, stylish afternoon tea (also at one time called low tea) should not be confused with high tea (also known as meat tea in the early days)—a robust, family meal of hearty, filling savory and sweet foods that was eaten at 5.30 or 6pm by the working classes when they returned from a long hard day in the factories, mines, and offices.

OPIUM WARS AND EMPIRE TEA

As tea consumption in Britain grew, annual imports from China were costing the country dear and China did not need or want the one export, cotton, that Britain had to offer. By 1800, opium had provided the answer to the problem. The Chinese wanted opium (despite its importation being banned by a Chinese law of 1727) and the British, and later the Portuguese, started adding to the local stock. The British East India Company grew the drug in Bengal (by then part of the British Empire), sold it, via wholesale merchants in Calcutta, to China for silver, then paid the same silver back to the Chinese for tea.

Despite more and more severe penalties from the Chinese government for the use and importation of opium, the illegal trade continued until, in 1839, a Chinese official, Lin Zexu, deposited 20,000 chests of it on

East India Company auction room.

the beach near Canton where a flood of sea water turned it into unusable sludge and washed it out to sea. A year later, Britain declared war on China and China retaliated by placing an embargo on all exports of tea.

In the light of the continuing difficulties in trade with China, Britain had, for some time, been considering other locations for the production of tea. Northern India was particularly promising because of the climate and altitudes and, when native trees were discovered growing in Upper Assam in 1823, small plantations were established by Charles Bruce, an employee of the British East India Company. He eventually persuaded his employers (who had persevered in their belief that only China seed was good enough) to cultivate the Assam variety of the tree on a commercial scale. The first shipment of Assam tea reached London in 1838, and the Assam Tea Company was set up in 1840 and soon expanded into Darjeeling, Cachar, Sylhet, and other North Indian areas.

In the 1870s, Ceylon also became a major British tea-producing area after the coffee crop failed in the 1860s and planters decided that tea was the most suitable alternative. One of the earliest planters was the Scot, James Taylor, whose pioneering efforts helped establish the crop as Ceylon's major export. Then, a visit to the island by a newcomer to the tea trade guaranteed its

Advertisement for Lipton's Ceylon teas.

success. At the age of 40, Thomas Lipton was already a millionaire from his grocery business—famous for its hams and cheeses, and with stores all over Britain and more than 70 in London alone. Lipton had always had a keen eye for business and, during a visit to the island's hill country, bought several plantations. He realized that by producing his own tea and marketing it direct to the British public in his own stores (thus cutting out the middle men), he could cut the cost of tea and still make a healthy profit. His slogan "Direct from the Tea Gardens to the Tea Pot" became famous and his colorful advertising campaigns ensured that the name of Lipton became synonymous with tea throughout the world.

Britain's consumption of tea rose from 23,730,000 pounds in 1801 to 258,847,000 in 1901, and imports of Indian and Ceylon teas gradually took over from China. Imports of mainly China teas reached a peak of 170 million pounds in 1886, then fell to 13 million pounds in 1900—only 7 percent of Britain's total imports. By 1939, China imports had fallen as low as 1.3 million pounds, However, by the 1970s, they had started to rise again and in 1978, Britain consumed 15 million pounds of China tea. Today, China's largest markets are Morocco and the U.S., the latter doubling its imports between 1978 and 1983, and still increasing its purchases today.

THE CLIPPER SHIPS

The ships of the East India Company generally took between 12 and 15 months to sail from China with their heavy cargos of tea and tea wares to the Port of London. In 1845, the first American clipper ship was launched and made the round trip from New York in less than eight months, posing a huge threat to British ship owners. In 1850, the first British clipper, the *Stornaway*, was built in Aberdeen and was followed by the launching of more of these sleek, yacht-like ships, some of which achieved record average speeds of up to 18 knots. The clippers

The tea clipper "Great Republic."

could each carry more than a million pounds of tea, the chests being intricately packed by native stevedores in the Chinese ports. The stability and solidity of the cargos helped increase the strength and performance of the ships so that monsoons, fast currents, reefs, storms, and attacks by pirates presented less of a danger on the voyages home.

Several clippers would set sail from China on the same tide and race back to London where bets were placed on who would win. A higher price was paid for the first tea home, and prizes were awarded to the winning crew. The most famous of the races was in 1866 when 40 vessels took part and headed for home, almost neck and neck. The *Aeriel*, the *Taeping*, and the *Serica* all docked on the same tide, 99 days after setting sail.

The last of the tea races was in 1871, by which date steamships had taken over the work of most of the clippers and the Suez Canal had opened, knocking several weeks off the voyage between Europe and Asia.

TEA-SHOPS AND TEA DANCES

After the closing of London's pleasure gardens, there was really nowhere to go for tea except home—until 1864, that is, when the manageress of the London Bridge branch of the Aerated Bread Company had the inspired idea of opening a room at the back of her store as a public tea-room. Her venture was so successful that other companies (selling a variety of products ranging from milk to tobacco, tea, and cakes) quickly copied her idea and suddenly, all over London and Britain's provincial towns, tea-shops opened. These popular establishments drew customers of all ages and from all classes. They served a variety of hot and cold, sweet and savory foods, cheap pots and cups of tea, and often provided music for the entertainment of the mixed clientele.

Going out to tea became a fashion that reached its heyday in the Edwardian period (1901–1914) when newly opened, exclusive hotels in London and elsewhere started serving stylish three-course afternoon teas in their lounges and palm courts, where string quartets and palm court trios created a calm and elegant atmosphere for their leisured patrons. In 1913, afternoon tea acquired a colorful additional element when the eccentric fashion for tea dances was born with the arrival of the sultry and risqué tango from Argentina. The trend for organizing dancing at teatime is thought to have originated in the French North African colonies and, as the tango, which had taken London's dance world by storm in 1910, became everyone's favorite, the two fashions coincided. Tango clubs, classes, and tea dances were organized all over London, in

The Tea House at College Farm, London.

theaters, restaurants, and hotels, and became the "place to be." London's newspapers reported the "Growing Craze for Tango Teas," announcing "Tango Teas for 1500" and "Everyone's Tangoing Now."

Changes in social patterns and life styles, due to the First and Second World Wars, the new trend among the smart set for cocktails rather than tea, and the onslaught, in the 1950s, of fast food outlets and coffee bars, led to a gradual decline in the fashion for going out to tea. The British continued, of course, to drink tea at home and in the workplace, but it was not until the early 1980s that there was a new surge of interest in tea and teatime that led to a revival of the British tea-shop, tea-room, and tea-lounge.

TEA IN NORTH AMERICA

It was inevitable that tea would find its way to North America with colonizing groups from Europe. New York (initially New Amsterdam under the Dutch and later renamed by the British) was a tea drinker's haven with all the same traditions and rules of etiquette, and the same favorite tea wares as in Britain, Holland, and Russia.

Chests of tea being thrown into Boston harbor.

Good quality drinking water was not readily available and so special water pumps were installed around Manhatten. Coffee houses and tea gardens became popular and New York had three Vauxhall Gardens, one Ranelagh, and others that took the same names as London's favorites.

In the cities, tea was drunk in the same elegant fashion as in Europe. In Philadelphia and Boston particularly, tea and expensive silver and porcelain were symbols of wealth and social status, and among less affluent families, the drinking of tea represented breeding and good manners.

In the early 1700s, the Quakers drank their "cups that cheer but not inebriate"

with salt and butter, while in New England, scented green China teas were popular. In rural areas, tea was brewed in a more simple rustic way and a pot kept hot on the stove all day, ready for pouring whenever visitors arrived or for the family when they came in from work in the fields.

The Boston Tea Party ended America's liking for both the British and their tea. The origins of the trouble lay in the passing of an Act of Parliament in 1767 which attempted to tax the American colonies. A 3 pence (2¢) in the pound duty on tea was to go toward the support of the army and government officials in the colonies and, since the only tea that could legally be imported and purchased in America was from the British East India Company, there seemed no way out of paying the new levy. Within two years of the passing of the act, most American ports were refusing to allow any dutiable goods ashore, and when the British sent seven shiploads of tea from London, feelings ran high. In New York and Philadelphia, demonstrations forced the ships to turn back, while in Charleston, customs officials seized the cargo. In Boston, general unrest over several weeks was followed by the boarding of the *Dartmouth* by a band of men disguised as Native Americans, to cries of "Boston harbor a teapot tonight" and "The Mowhawks are coming." In the course of the next three hours, they threw 340 chests of tea overboard. The British government's closure of Boston harbor and the arrival of British troops on American soil marked the beginning of the War of Independence and America's coffee-drinking tradition.

WHAT'S IN A NAME?

Until the name "tea" was accepted into the English language, the leaf was variously called *tcha*, *cha*, *tay* and *tee*. The English name derived, not from the standard Mandarin Chinese word, *cha*, but from the Chinese Amoy dialect name *te* (pronounced tay). This resulted from the early contact between the Dutch traders and Chinese junks out of the port of Amoy in China's Fujian Province. The name became *thee* in Dutch and, since it was the Dutch who were mainly responsible for transporting the first tea to Europe, the new product also became known as *thee* in German, *te* in Italian, Spanish, Danish, Norwegian, Swedish, Hungarian, and Malay, *tea* in English, *thé* in French, *tee* in Finnish, *teja* in Latvian, *ta* in Korean, *tey* in Tamil, *thay* in Sinhalese, and *Thea* to scientists.

The Mandarin, *cha*, became *ch'a* in Cantonese and passed as *cha* to Portuguese (during trade at Cantonese-speaking Macao) and so also to Persian, Japanese, and Hindi, becoming *shai* in Arabic, *ja* in Tibetan, *chay* in Turkish, and *chai* in Russian.

P R O D U C T I O N
O F   T E A

THE TEA PLANT

T EA (*THEA SINENSIS*) IS AN EVERGREEN plant of the Camellia family. Three closely related varieties are generally recognized by botanists—tea from China, Assam, and Cambodia—and all are used in commercial production.

Camellia sinensis, the China bush, can grow to a maximum height of 9–15 feet, and thrives in China, Tibet, and Japan. It can withstand very cold temperatures and can go on producing its 2 inch long leaves for up to 100 years. *Camellia assamica* is considered to be a tree rather than a bush and can reach heights of 45–60 feet, with leaves that range between 6–14 inches in length. It flourishes in tropical climates and goes on producing for approximately 40 years. The Cambodian variety *Camellia assamica subspecies lasiocalyx* is also a tree that grows to about 15 feet, and is used mainly in the production of hybrids.

The plant produces dark green, shiny, leathery leaves and delicate, small, white blossoms approximately 1 inch in diameter, with five or seven petals, rather like those of the jasmine flower. These produce a nutmeg-like fruit that contains from one to three seeds. Tea plants grow best in hot and humid conditions. The most suitable climates offer temperatures ranging from 50°–85°F, 80–90 inches of rainfall a year, and elevations from 1,000–7,000 feet above sea level. A combination of altitude and humidity promotes the desired slow growth, and the higher the tea is grown, the more flavor it has

The delicate flower of the thea sinensis.

and the finer the quality. Many of the world's most famous teas—high-grown Ceylons, China's Weyi, India's best Darjeelings—come from bushes cultivated above 4,000 feet.

As with the production of wine, the final taste and quality of the product are influenced by many important contributory factors—climate, soil, altitude, conditions, when and how it is plucked and processed, the blending, packaging, transportation, and storage.

THE CHEMISTRY OF TEA

The leaves of the *Camellia sinensis* contain a number of chemicals (including amino-acids, carbohydrates, mineral ions, caffeine, and polyphenolic compounds) which give the tea its characteristic color and flavor. They also contain 75–80 percent water which, during the first withering stages of the manufacturing process, is reduced to 60–70 percent. During the fermentation (or oxidation) stage of oolong and black tea processing, the polyphenolic flavanols (or catechins) oxidize with oxygen in the air to create the unique flavor and color of the infused liquor. The firing (or drying) process deactivates the enzyme that causes the oxidation and also further reduces the water content to approximately 3 percent.

The aroma of black tea is extremely complex. More than 550 chemicals have so far been identified, including hydrocarbons, alcohols, and acids. Most of these are formed during the manufacturing process and each chemical adds its own important qualities to the flavor of the tea through the drinker's sense of smell. The taste, however, mainly results from the various polyphenolic compounds (popularly but incorrectly called tannins) modified by caffeine.

Caffeine is one of the most important constituents of tea. It acts as a mild stimulant and increases activity of the digestive juices. All types of tea—green, oolong, and black—contain caffeine, but in different quantities. Green tea has less than oolong, and oolong less than black. It is generally estimated that an average cup of green tea contains 8.36 mg of caffeine, oolong tea has 12.55 mg, and black tea 25–110 mg, whereas an average cup of coffee contains 60–120 mg. Therefore, those worried about their caffeine intake should drink the paler, lighter brews from green or oolong teas. It is also worth noting that, whereas the caffeine in coffee is absorbed rapidly into the body, thus stimulating an immediate increase in blood circulation and cardio-vascular activity, the polyphenols in tea are thought to slow down the rate of absorption. The effects of the caffeine are felt more slowly but remain in the body for longer, thus making tea a much more re-freshing and revitalizing beverage than coffee.

HOW THE TEA GROWS

In the past, tea plants were normally grown from seed, but today's new stock is being produced more and more by vegetative propagation (from cuttings and from layered transplanted rooted branches) and from clonal leaf cuttings. By cloning the plants that produce well and withstand drought, pests, and diseases, producers are aiming for consistency of crop quality and increased commercial viability of their plantations.

New plants are raised in a tea nursery and transplanted to the plantation after about six months, by which time they have grown to a height of approximately 6–8 inches. The young bushes are each allowed approximately 16 square feet in which to grow and are left unplucked and unpruned for two years or so, during which period they reach a height of about 5–6 feet. They are then pruned back to about 1 foot high, allowed to grow a little, then pruned weekly to keep them at waist height. Commercial plucking begins after three to five years, depending on the altitude and conditions.

In some parts of the world, the plants go on growing throughout the year, while in others there is a dormant winter period and a growing period. The leaves are plucked as the new shoots—or "flush"—are beginning to grow. In hotter conditions, the plants have several flushes, while in cooler climates, there is a shorter, limited flushing season. Leaves from the early flushes are widely sought after, but it is the second flushes that are considered to give the finest teas. For the best quality tea, pickers remove two leaves and a bud from each new shoot. These are nipped off with a downward movement of

the thumb and then placed in bags or baskets carried by each plucker.

Because of a shortage of labor in some tea-producing areas, mechanical plucking, carried out with specially adapted tractors and harvesters or with hand-held shears, has replaced the traditional, very skilled hand-plucking, but the quality of the tea is inevitably inferior. However, teas produced in this way are useful for blending, and continuing research is attempting to improve mechanical methods.

Opposite top: New plants in a tea nursery.

Opposite bottom: Pruning a young tea bush.

Above: The buds and leaves are plucked and then carried in baskets to a collection point to be weighed.

TEA PROCESSING

It was thought at one time that green and black teas were made from different plants, but it is, in fact, only the different processing methods that produce the six main different types—white, green, oolong, black, scented, and compressed—and the many different varieties within each category, making a total of more than 3,000 teas from around the world.

WHITE TEA

This is produced on a very limited scale in China (originally in Fujian Province) and Sri Lanka. The new buds are plucked before they open, are withered to allow the natural moisture to evaporate, and then dried. The curled-up buds have a silvery appearance (and are sometimes referred to as Silver Tip) and give a very pale, straw-colored liquor.

GREEN TEA

Green teas are often referred to as "non-fermented" or "unfermented" teas. The freshly picked leaves are allowed to dry, then are heat-treated to stop any fermentation (or oxidation) that would rot the leaf. In China, traditional hand-making methods are still employed in many places, particularly in the manufacture of China's finest teas, but some factories have introduced a mechanized process. By the traditional method, the fresh green leaves are spread out in a thin layer on bamboo trays and exposed to sunlight or natural warm air for one or two hours. The leaves are then placed, a small amount at a time, into hot roasting pans and moved about quickly with the hands, as they become moist and soft and the natural moisture evaporates. (A small amount of China's green teas are steamed rather than roasted.) After four or five minutes, the softened leaves are rolled into balls on bamboo tables (in the larger factories, this

Pai Mu Tan Imperial from China.

Matcha Uji, a Japanese powdered green tea.

was traditionally done with the feet) and the tea balls are then again placed almost immediately into the hot roasting pans and moved about rapidly before being rolled for a second time or being left to dry. After one or two hours, the leaves have turned a dull green and undergo no further change. They are finally sifted to separate them into different-size pieces of leaf.

In Japan, the plucked leaves are steamed quickly on a moving belt, making them supple and soft ready for rolling. They are cooled and then repeatedly rolled, twisted, and dried until all the moisture has evaporated. A final rolling stage shapes and styles the leaves before the last drying period. The tea is then allowed to cool before being packed into airtight containers for shipment to retail stores. Some Japanese teas are still processed by hand, although most factories are now mechanized.

OOLONG TEAS

Oolong tea is generally referred to as "semi-fermented" tea and is principally manufactured in China and Taiwan (still known as Formosa in tea terminology).

For the manufacture of China oolongs, the leaves must not be picked too soon and it is important that they are processed immediately after plucking. They are first wilted in direct sunlight, then shaken in bamboo baskets to lightly bruise the edges of

A China oolong tea, Fenghuang Dancong.

the leaves. Next, they are alternately shaken and spread out to dry until the surface of the leaf turns slightly yellow. The edges turn a reddish color as the chemicals in the bruised leaf react with oxygen. This fermentation or oxidation period (12–20 percent fermentation) is halted after 1½–2 hours by firing. Oolongs are always whole leaf teas, never broken by rolling. Formosa oolongs undergo a longer fermentation period (60–70 percent) and are therefore blacker in appearance than China oolongs, and give a richer, darker liquor than the paler orangy-brown infusion of China oolong.

Pouchong is another variety of very lightly fermented tea that undergoes a shorter fermentation than oolongs and almost forms an extra category somewhere between green and oolong. Pouchongs originated in Fujian Province but most are now made in Taiwan and are often used as a base for Jasmine tea and other scented teas.

BLACK TEA

Methods and varieties differ considerably between the different producing regions, but the process always involves four basic steps—withering, rolling, fermenting, and firing (or drying). For the traditional "orthodox" method (still used in China, Taiwan, parts of India, Sri Lanka, Indonesia, and elsewhere) which produces larger particles of leaf, the plucked leaves are spread out to wither (in the shade for finer varieties) until limp enough to be rolled without splitting the surface of the leaf. At this stage, the leaves give out a fruity, almost apple-like odor. Next, the withered leaf is rolled, in order to release the chemicals within the leaf that are essential to the final color and flavor. This is still done by hand in some factories, but most use Rotorvane machines to crush the leaf lightly. The rolled lumps of tea are then broken up and the leaf spread out in a cool, humid atmosphere for 3½–4½ hours to absorb oxygen, which causes a chemical change in the leaf particles and turns them from green to a coppery red.

Finally, the oxidized (or fermented) leaf is fired in order to arrest the natural

Ndu tea from Cameroon.

decomposition and, at this stage, the particles turn black and acquire their recognizable tea smell. Firing was traditionally carried out in large pans over open fires and this method is still used in some Chinese factories, but most producers now pass the tea through hot air tunnels or bake it in hot ovens.

The CTC method (cut, tear, and curl) produces smaller leaf particles that give a stronger, quicker brew, making them ideal for use in tea bags. The withered leaf is passed through the rollers of a CTC machine which rotate at different speeds, or an LTP (Lawrie Tea Processor) rotating hammer-mill leaf disintegrator, which tears and breaks it into tiny particles. The rest of the process is the same as for orthodox black teas.

PRODUCTION OF BLACK TEA

The leaves are spread out on long trays.

An orthodox rolling machine lightly breaks the leaves.

Broken leaves are laid out to "ferment" or "oxidize."

As the leaves dry they change from rusty brown to black.

The CTC machine cuts and tears the leaves into small fragments.

SCENTED TEAS

Green, oolong, and black teas are all used to make scented teas. The additional flavorings are mixed with the processed leaf as a final stage before the tea is packed. For Jasmine tea, whole jasmine blossoms are added to green or black tea, for Rose Pouchong or Rose Congou, rose petals are blended with China or Formosa oolong or black leaf. Fruit-flavored teas are generally made by blending the fruits' essential oils with the processed tea. Herbal, fruit, and flower tisanes and infusions that do not contain any product of the *Camellia sinensis* should not be confused with scented and flavored teas. These herbals are not teas and should not be labeled as such.

Orchid scented tea from China.

COMPRESSED TEAS

Chinese tea producers first started forming their tea into solid cakes during the days of the Tang Dynasty by first steaming the green leaves and then compressing them into cakes or bricks that were then allowed to dry. China's modern tea bricks consist of tea dust that has been hydraulically compressed into slabs weighing just over 2 pounds. Also available today are small seven-layer cakes, balls of tea, and nest-shaped and bowl-shaped compressed teas. Pu'erh teas are sold for their medicinal qualities and are thought to be extremely good for the digestion, treating diarrhea, indigestion, and high cholesterol levels.

A China compressed tea, Tuocha Lubao.

METHODS OF PRODUCTION

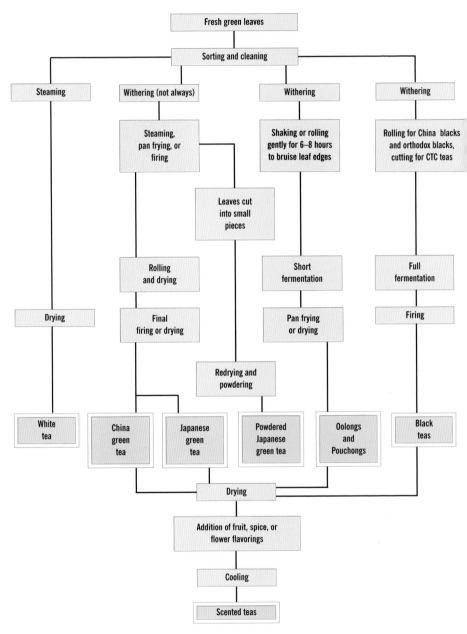

ORGANIC TEA

The organic production of tea is a relatively new development—dating back only seven to ten years. Cultivation under organic rules is extremely complicated and rigidly controlled. All fertilizers, pesticides, and herbicides must be absolutely free of chemicals and must rely totally on substances such as dung, compost, natural organic matter, and plants and trees that provide necessary nutrients, ground cover, etc. The aims of organic estates are to achieve long-term sustainability of soil fertility and productivity, protect the environment, and create a form of organic micro-system that produces an economically viable tea that is totally free of chemicals.

This does not imply that all non-organic teas contain chemicals, but rather that an organic system produces tea for a growing market of consumers who care about the environment and the long-term health of the planet, and which recognizes and appreciates the fine quality and flavor of some of the organic teas being produced today in India, Africa, and Sri Lanka. Makaibari in Darjeeling was certified by the Organic Farmers and Growers, UK, in 1990 and produces highly acclaimed teas of exceptional quality. Mullootor is another Darjeeling garden that went organic in 1986, and Lonrho, in Tanzania, has been producing organic tea, since 1989. Their product has even been drunk at Buckingham Palace. In Sri Lanka, Needwood Estate is now also producing organic teas.

Spreading organic fertilizer on a tea plantation in Tanzania.

TEA LEAF GRADES

The final stage in the tea process is the sorting, or grading, of the leaf. As the leaf particles emerge from the dryers or ovens, they are passed through sifters with graduated mesh sizes to divide them into different-size pieces. Experts make their classification, not according to quality or taste, but by the appearance and type of the pieces of leaf. However, the finest grades almost inevitably also give the finest quality. The two main divisions are "leaf" grades and "broken" grades, the leaf grades consisting of the larger pieces that are left after the broken grades have been sifted out.

Grading is a crucial stage in the tea-making process because when brewing, strength, flavor, and color infuse from the leaf into the boiling water at different rates according to leaf size—the larger the leaf, the slower the rate of infusion, and vice versa. It is important that all pieces of leaf used for one pot of tea are the same size. In the blending of different teas, each packet must contain regular-size particles, since smaller pieces will sink to the bottom and cause an imbalance in the carefully created blend.

Grading terminology is concerned with the size of the leaf, so it follows that different-size pieces of the same tea will be of equal quality—the only difference being that smaller leaf particles will brew more quickly. Within each grade of tea from a particular garden there may be variations in quality (and therefore in price) due to the weather or the production process, and tea buyers have to taste a number of different teas before making their choice. A number 1 is often added after the grading letters to denote absolutely top quality tea.

The sorting machine separates the leaves into different grades.

GRADING TERMINOLOGY

Leaf grades are divided into the following categories:

Flowery Orange Pekoe (FOP)
This denotes tea made from the end bud and first leaf of each shoot. FOP contains fine, tender young leaves rolled with the correct proportion of tip, the delicate end pieces of the buds, that guarantee quality.

Golden Flowery Orange Pekoe (GFOP)
This is FOP with "golden tips"—the very ends of the golden yellow buds.

Tippy Golden Flowery Orange Pekoe (TGFOP) This is FOP with a large proportion of golden tips.

Finest Tippy Golden Flowery Orange Pekoe (FTGFOP) This is exceptionally high quality FOP.

Special Finest Tippy Golden Flowery Orange Pekoe (SFTGFOP) This is the very best FOP.

Orange Pekoe (OP) This contains long, pointed leaves that are larger than in FOP and have been harvested when the end buds open into leaf. OP seldom contains "tips".

Pekoe (P) This consists of shorter, less fine leaves than OP.

Flowery Pekoe (FP) The leaves for FP are rolled into balls.

Pekoe Souchong (PS) This consists of shorter, coarser leaves than P.

Souchong (S) Large leaves are rolled, lengthwise, producing coarse, ragged pieces. The term is often used for China's smoked teas.

Broken leaf grades are divided into the following categories:

Golden Flowery Broken Orange Pekoe (GFBOP), Golden Broken Orange Pekoe (GBOP), Tippy Golden Broken Orange Pekoe (TGBOP), Tippy Golden Flowery Broken Orange Pekoe (TGFBOP), Flowery Broken Orange Pekoe (FBOP), Broken Orange Pekoe (BOP), Broken Pekoe (BP), Broken Pekoe Souchong (BPS)
Fannings/Fines (also referred to as Dusts) Fannings are made up of the finest siftings and are useful in blends for tea bags which require a quick brew. A number 1 is also added to broken leaf grades to denote the best quality. Dusts and fannings are further categorized as:
Orange Fannings (OF), Broken Orange Pekoe Fannings (BOPF), Pekoe Fannings (PF), Broken Pekoe Fannings (BPF), Pekoe Dust, Red Dust (RD), Fine Dust (FD), Golden Dust (GD), Super Red Dust (SRD), Super Fine Dust (SFD), Broken Mixed Fannings (BMF)

Tea Blends

After the various stages of the manufacturing process, teas are either packed and marketed as "specialty" teas (also referred to as "single source" or "garden" teas) or they are blended with teas from other gardens or other producing areas or countries. This is because teas from single estates or plantations can, like wines, vary from year to year in flavor and quality, due to annual and seasonal variations in weather patterns and, sometimes, in production processes. This means that, for example, a 1996 Broken Orange Pekoe from Diyagama

Skilled blending ensures consistency of flavor.

Estate in Sri Lanka may be different from the same grade from the same garden in 1997. Some connoisseurs prefer to only buy single source teas and enjoy these subtle variations from year to year. Other tea drinkers like to know that each time they buy a particular tea —for example, Darjeeling Second Flush, Ceylon BOP, English Breakfast—the brew will taste exactly the same. By blending together a number of different teas, packaging companies and retailers can guarantee the flavor and quality of that tea from year to year.

Tea blending is a work of art. Tea tasters sample hundreds of teas each day to find the necessary components for a particular blend and each blend may contain 15–35 different teas. Bulk blending to a given recipe is carried out in large drums to ensure even mixing before the contents are packaged into tea bags, packages, or caddies.

The Art of the Tea Taster

Tea tasting is an essential part of the work of both tea brokers and tea blenders. Brokers taste teas in order to assess their value prior to auction, blenders decide which individual teas are needed for a standard blend. It takes at least five years to train as a tea taster and most will tell you that even after 40 or so years in the trade, they are still learning.

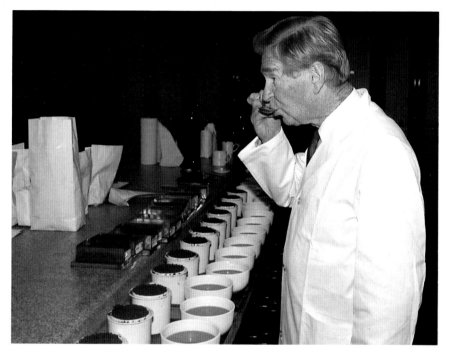

The tea taster slurps the tea sharply into his mouth.

To prepare teas for tasting, the dry leaves are laid in containers in rows on the tasting bench. A specific weight of each tea is then placed in a special lidded brewing mug and boiling water is poured on. The brewing is very carefully timed, usually 5 or 6 minutes. The brew is then poured into tasting bowls and the infused leaf tipped on to the lid of the brewing mug. Tasters in the U.K. usually also add a specific amount of milk since most blends for the British market are designed to be drunk with milk. The taster works in much the same way as a wine taster. He slurps the tea sharply into his mouth so that it hits the taste buds, then he rolls the liquid around in the mouth to assess the flavor before spitting it out into a special mobile spittoon that can be rolled alongside the tasting table or bench. The taster also takes into account the appearance of the dry leaf, the infused leaf, and the color and quality of the liquor.

TEA TASTER'S VOCABULARY

Tasters and blenders have a vocabulary of some hundred words to describe appearance and flavor. The most common are:

body—a tea with body has a strong liquor not a thin, weak one

bold—big pieces of leaf

brassy—refers to a liquor with a bitter taste

bright—a bright liquor, not dull in appearance

brisk—a lively taste, a well-fermented, well-fired tea

choppy—leaf that has been chopped in a breaker or cutter rather than rolled

coarse—a liquor that has strength but poor quality

colory—special category teas with good colored liquor

dull—the opposite of bright, and not a desirable quality

even—leaf pieces of roughly the same size

flaky—leaf that is in flakes rather than twisted pieces

flat—a tea that has gone off, has too much moisture

flavory—with a distinctive taste

grainy—denotes well-made fannings or dusts

gray—gray-colored leaf resulting from over-cutting or because the desirable coating of juices on the leaf has been rubbed off due to over-handling during the sifting stage

greenish—an infusion with a bright green color, not desirable, due to under-rolling or under-fermentation

harsh—a bitter, raw taste with little strength

irregular—uneven-size pieces of leaf

malty—with a hint of malt, found in well-made teas

mellow—the opposite of greenish, harsh, etc

point—leaf with desirable briskness

plain—lacking in desirable qualities

pungent—astringent without being bitter

ragged—uneven and irregular pieces of leaf

smooth—with a pleasant, rounded taste

tainted—unpleasant flavor caused by chemicals used in cultivation, or by damp conditions, or by pollution during transportation, etc

thin—a tea with little strength due to hard withering, under-rolling, or too high a temperature during rolling

tip—the very end of the delicate young buds that give golden flecks to the processed leaf

wiry—well-twisted leaf, as opposed to open pieces

TEA TRADE

Until the 1840s, when the clipper ships were built, it took between 15 and 18 months to sail stocks of tea from China and Java back to London. The great clipper tea races attracted huge publicity and added excitement and color to a very everyday commodity. Today, tea is transported from plantation to consumer far less glamorously, in vast containers that are filled in the producing country (sometimes at the estates but more often in the docks), loaded on to container ships, and sailed to consumer countries. Careful handling and dry, secure storage are still crucial in the transportation of bulk tea, and improvements are being made all the time at all levels—from estate and factory to bulk shipping and warehousing companies.

In the early days, all tea was sold to merchant shippers who transported the tea home and offered it for sale by auction. England's earliest recorded sale took place in London on March 11, 1679, and by the mid-eighteenth century, quarterly auctions of China tea were being held. In 1861, the first Indian auctions were held in Calcutta and since then, auction centers have been established in most countries of origin—Colombo in 1883, Chittagong in 1949, Nairobi in 1957, etc. Offshore auctions were introduced in 1982 and helped solve the problem involved in the landed auctions, of long delays in transferring money from purchaser to broker.

Loading tea onto a container ship.

Today, approximately 50 percent of the world's tea production is sold through public auction—China teas being the only ones not offered in this way. Prior to an auction, a small hole is bored in each tea chest or sack and samples are sent to the world's leading tea buyers. If a buyer likes the sample he has tasted, he will bid for it at the auction. Sometimes, as many as 50,000 chests (5,000,000 pounds) of tea are sold in one day in this way. The highest bidder then either ships the tea he has bought to fill an order, or he sends samples to importers around the world. Eventually, the shipments travel from the country of origin to the importing countries. Modern changes in the trade may eventually lead to the introduction of electronic on-screen auctions whereby buyers will be able to "attend" direct from their offices all over the world instead of having to be personally present in the auction room.

PACKAGING

Until 1368, China tea, in the form of compressed cakes and bricks, was easy to store and transport. The solid slabs neither disintegrated nor lost their flavor. However, the change during the Ming Dynasty to loose leaf tea created new problems of storage and transportation. The leaves were carried in bamboo baskets (which cannot have protected the fine flavor), sealed in earthenware jars (which were extremely heavy), or in laquered chests. As trade with Europe and America developed in the early seventeenth century, jars and baskets were no longer practical and were replaced by ordinary wooden chests. Common varieties of tea were packed into bamboo crates lined with wax paper, rice paper, bamboo paper, or mulberry paper. Finer quality teas were packed into decorated laquer chests and the general rule was the finer the tea, the smaller the chest.

When Britain started producing tea in Assam, chests were manufactured in Rangoon from special kits that included planks cut to the requisite length, lead sheets to form a lining, and sheets of silver foil to cover the tea. To help settle the tea and therefore pack it more tightly, the chests were rocked on a split bamboo cane or pressed down with the feet. These primitive methods were later replaced by machinery that vibrated the chests in order to shake the tea down. The lead lining was later thought to contaminate the tea and was replaced with aluminum foil.

Tea chests are used less and less today, but are still essential for the transportation of expensive, larger leaf teas that would easily break up in the paper sacks that have replaced the chests. The sacks are made from layers of tough paper with a layer of

Chests are used for transporting large-leaf teas.

aluminum foil as the innermost ply, protecting the tea from odors and moisture. Empty sacks are delivered to tea estates around the world and, once filled, are loaded on to pallets and containerized ready for shipping. Paper sacks have made the transportation of teas easier, lighter, and more efficient, but also, importantly, they are helping ecologically by reducing the need for timber and because the used sacks are recyclable.

Until the 1820s, once the tea had reached the European retailer, it was sold loose, and customers could buy as much or as little as they wanted in a screw of paper. Merchants sold "straights", or blended tea to clients' requirements. In 1826, the first pre-packaged tea was introduced by John Horniman in an effort to encourage customers to buy tea by name—his name—rather than whatever tea the retailer had in stock. His idea did not catch on until the 1880s, when most companies took to marketing their teas in this way and became involved in elaborate advertising campaigns that offered all sorts of extra gifts—from free pianos to widows' pensions—with purchases of tea.

Today, pre-packed teas are available in a wide variety of cardboard packages, (some designed to replace the caddy on the kitchen shelf), decorative tins, and wooden boxes. Some companies are also vacuum-packing their tea in the country of origin in order to further reduce the risk of pollution and deterioration of the product.

Transfair International logo.

FAIR TRADE TEA

The concept of Fair Trade attempts to address the imbalance between the wages paid to workers, particularly in the Third World, who produce the tea and the money made by those who trade in it. By the Fair Trade system, traders purchase direct from small producer groups and sell through mail-order catalogs and special retail outlets. Money earned by the producers goes toward improving the quality of life for workers through such schemes as pension funds, alternative training opportunities, environmental improvements, and welfare and medical programs. For example, in 1995, the first Fair Trade premiums reached Ambootia

Tea Estate in Darjeeling, India, where in 1968, a part of the plantation crashed into the valley below. The money is attempting to arrest the landslide (the biggest in South Asia) and prevent the destruction that poses such an enormous threat to the garden, to the local environment, and to the economic stability of the plantation workers.

Fair Trade teas from various approved sources in Darjeeling, Assam, Southern India, Sri Lanka, Nepal, Tanzania, and Zimbabwe are available in a number of countries, including Germany, Switzerland, Italy, Luxemburg, the U.K., The Netherlands, Austria, Canada, Japan, and the U.S., and now also appear in the Oxfam catalog.

WORLD TRENDS IN THE TEA INDUSTRY

In the last 30 or 40 years, tea production has expanded by 156 percent, and 1995 saw a record crop of 2,854,982 tons, 2 percent up on 1994. This is mainly the result of improved production methods, innovative planting techniques, the breeding of selected clonal plants, improved pest and disease controls, new machinery, and advances in tea sciences and technology. Alongside the increased rate of production, the steady decline of tea prices since 1963 has led to problems in some producing countries where rising costs of production are not offset by profits.

There are fluctuations in the output of individual countries depending on weather patterns, political and economic stability, and the individual country's commitment to tea production. Some countries, notably Mauritius, Uganda, and China, are currently reducing their production.

Import and export patterns have also changed significantly over the last 30 or 40 years, with demand from the U.K. showing a downward trend. Britain is the biggest consumer of tea after Ireland, but in 1995, imports were 8 percent down on the previous year. This was blamed partly on a very hot summer. And in the U.S., the total of 89,618 tons imported was 16 percent lower than in 1994. This was partly due to over-optimistic predictions of demand for ready-to-drink bottled and canned teas in 1994.

Pakistan, Russia, and other C.I.S. countries increased their total imports due, in the case of the latter two, to economic recovery and favorable commercial conditions provided by the exporting countries. And increased domestic consumption in India, China, and other Asian countries has contributed to a stronger demand in some sectors of the market. Western Europe has also increased its importation of tea due to a wider and growing interest in tea drinking, particularly in Germany and France.

The tea market in all countries faces constant competition from coffee and soft drinks. But among tea drinkers in such countries as the U.K., the U.S., and Japan, there is an increasing awareness of different types of tea and a growing demand for a wider variety of good quality specialty teas.

The tea trade is optimistic that current research programs into the health benefits of tea consumption will produce results that will encourage consumers to increase their tea intake. The media is already reporting the fact that tea can help reduce the risk of stroke and thrombosis, and further results of experiments are expected to provide a positive message that will lead to an increased world-wide demand for all types of tea.

TEA EQUIPAGE

BREWING VESSELS

I N THE EARLIEST CHINESE HISTORY OF TEA DRINKING, leaves were boiled in water in open pans. But the Ming Dynasty fashion for steeping processed leaves in hot water created the need for a covered vessel in which to infuse the leaves and to keep the liquor hot. Ewers, that resembled a modern teapot, had been used for wine for centuries in China and these were adapted to tea brewing.

Gradually the idea of the teapot evolved and by the time the Dutch started carrying cargos of tea back to Europe from China in the late sixteenth century, the teapots they included in their purchases were small, broad-based, and squat with wide spouts that did not easily clog with leaves. The Chinese stoneware was new to Europe, and it took Dutch potters until the late 1670s to duplicate the heat-resistant pots. Two of the

Chinese porcelain, c. 1690.

Meissen, c. 1740.

English silver, 1729.

successful potters from The Netherlands, the Elers brothers, took their craft to England, settled in Staffordshire, and established the English pottery industry.

Just as Europeans had never seen stoneware like that produced in China, neither had they ever dreamt of the fine translucent pottery known as porcelain that had been invented by the Chinese under the Tang Dynasty. It took the Elers brothers and other European potters almost a hundred years to discover the secret of manufacturing genuine hard-paste porcelain and bone china. British potters started creating stoneware, porcelain, and bone china tea wares in the eighteenth century when names such as Wedgwood, Spode, Worcester, Minton, and Derby became famous. Whereas these early manufacturers found it difficult to

produce larger plates and dishes that did not warp or break in the firing process, the smaller items needed for tea were more easily and very successfully produced.

The size and shape of teapots over the years has changed to suit tastes and fashions. Early pots followed the Chinese tradition for using mythological symbols and creatures. Later pots reflected eighteenth-century rococo or neo-classical shapes and the heavily ornamented styles of nineteenth-century Victoriana. Today, pots are available in every possible shape and size—large or small, simple, practical, ornate, with infusers or without. They also come in every possible form—from animals, birds, and plants to pieces of furniture, vehicles, characters from literature, and personalities from show business and public life.

Staffordshire china, c. 1900.

Coalport, c. 1800-5.

Noritake, c. 1930.

THE INFUSER POT

There are several elegant glass pots on the market today which have their own in-built infuser sitting in the neck of the pot. To brew the tea, warm the pot in the usual way, measure the leaves into the infuser and pour on the boiling water. Put on the lid and leave to brew for the required number of minutes. Lift out the infuser with the leaves as soon as the tea has reached the desired strength.

Above: Jena glass teapot and warming stand, admired so much for its design that it is on display at the Museum of Modern Art, New York.

Below: Modern infuser pot and tea glass.

TEAPOT WITH PLUNGER

The thinking behind this style of pot is to isolate the leaves after infusion in the same way that coffee is isolated in a cafetière. Once the tea has reached the desired strength, the plunger is depressed to shut off any contact between the leaves and hot water. This stops any more tea solubles from being released into the water. The advantage over the infuser pot is that there is no risk of mess caused by a dripping infuser as it is removed from the pot.

Teapot with infuser and plunger.

INFUSERS

Traditional teapots do not often have their own infusers and there are a number of infusers on the market made for use in any style of pot, or for use in cups or mugs. These come in a variety of sizes and are made from different materials. Avoid one-cup infusers since these do not give the tea leaves enough room to infuse properly. Larger leaf teas sometimes expand to several times the size of the dry leaf when infused in boiling water and unless they have room to do this, the tea solubles that give the brew its flavor cannot pass from leaf to water.

Teaball infuser

Mesh teaball

Spoon infuser

Muslin infuser

Spring-handled
infuser

Swiss gold tea filter

Mesh pot infuser

Porcelain mugs with infusers.

INFUSER MUGS

Infuser mugs are an excellent way to brew an individual serving of tea. The idea is based on the Chinese covered brewing cup, *guywan*, but recognizes the fact that it is better to remove black and oolong leaves from the boiling water once the liquor has brewed to the desired strength. The generous size of the infuser ensures that the leaves have plenty of room to infuse properly.

Warm the infuser mug with boiling water before brewing the tea in the usual way (see page 76). Place the appropriate amount of leaf into the infuser and then pour on boiling water for oolong and black tea, and just under boiling for green or white teas. Once the infusion is ready, lift out the infuser.

THE GUYWAN (Chinese Covered Cup)

The *guywan* (Mandarin for covered cup, "zhong" or "cha chung" in Cantonese) has been used in China since about 1350. It consists of saucer, bowl, and lid which are designed to be used together. To brew black or oolong tea in the traditional Chinese fashion, first place the tea in the bottom of

Chinese guywan.

the *guywan*. Pour in enough boiling water to come just under halfway up the cup and immediately drain off by holding the cup and saucer together and using the lid as a strainer to hold back the leaves. Now uncover the leaves and inhale the aroma from the "rinsed" leaves. If brewing green tea, omit this first step and proceed directly to the next stage.

Next, pour fresh boiling water into the *guywan*, not directly on to the leaves but down the inside of the cup to set the leaves swirling in the bottom. For green tea, leave the cup uncovered, infuse for two or three minutes, and then drink. For black or oolong tea, cover the cup with the lid and leave to infuse for the required number of minutes (see individual entries in the directory).

To drink from the *guywan*, hold the saucer in the palm of the right hand, using the thumb to steady the cup. With your left hand, lift the lid by the knob, tilting it slightly away from you so that it holds back the leaves while you sip the liquor. Before drinking all the liquor, add more hot water, again down the inside of the cup rather than directly on to the leaves, to draw out more of the tea's flavor. A third addition of water may be made directly on to the leaves. Go on drinking and adding more water as many times as yields a good flavor from the leaves.

THE YIXING TEAPOT

Fine pottery has been made at Yixing since 2500 B.C. A monk at a nearby temple is said to have created the first *zisha* (purple sand), unglazed Yixing teapot in the early 1500s. The stoneware was found to keep tea hotter than porcelain, and the reddish-brown or green pots became very popular both in China and Japan. They were produced in all sorts of fanciful shapes—lotus flower, narcissus, fruits, bamboo trunk—or in starkly simple forms that allowed the beauty of the stoneware to speak for itself.

Tea aficionados still prize Yixing pots today. The unglazed stoneware is thought to bring out the flavor of fine Chinese teas. A new pot needs a little time to acquire a lining which will give its own seasoned flavor to the tea, and should be kept for one sort of tea only. Brew the tea in the usual way, following the Golden Rules (see page 76).

Chinese Yixing red stoneware teapot decorated with enameled flowers and prunus root.

JAPANESE TEA BOWLS

The large tea bowls used for powdered green tea drinking in Japan come in a variety of shapes. Ideally the bowl should be relatively thick (if it is too thick, it does not get warm enough; if too thin, it becomes too hot to hold), with a soft, smooth, comfortable feel to the outside. It should be wide enough so that the bamboo whisk can be freely and effectively used. Raku wares, made in Japan, are thought to fulfill all the requirements of a green tea bowl, and bowls made in Korea, originally meant for rice, also have a pleasant softness to the touch and are very suitable.

To brew powdered green tea, place a generous ½ teaspoon of Matcha (Japanese powdered green tea) in a bowl and gently pour on 8 teaspoons water at a temperature of 185°F. Whisk quickly and lightly with a bamboo whisk, a *chasen*, to make the frothy, rich liquor.

Japanese bowl and whisk to be used for making powdered tea.

TEA COZIES

Tea cozies need very careful use. If placed over a pot of tea that contains tea leaves and hot water, the tea is likely to overbrew and taste "stewed" or bitter. It is much better to brew the tea using an infuser, remove the infuser and leaves when the liquor has reached a perfect strength, and then cover the pot with a cozy. Alternatively, strain the infused tea into a second warmed pot and cover with a cozy.

Some teapot manufacturers still make the attractive style of pot that was very popular in the 1930s and 40s—the "Cosiware" pot—which has an infuser that sits neatly in the neck of the pot and lifts out easily, and a fitted jacket of insulated chrome which ensures that the tea keeps beautifully hot.

CADDIES AND CADDY SPOONS

The first containers used for the domestic storage of tea were the jars and bottles that arrived from China with shipments of tea. They were usually small, round-bellied, covered jars, often in typical oriental blue and white porcelain, with cup-shaped lids that were used to measure the tea leaves into the pot. Gradually, European jars and boxes were developed in a wide range of shapes and sizes—round, square, and cylindrical boxes, jars and bottles, in silver, crystal, stoneware, and wood.

The word "caddy" was not used until the end of the eighteenth century when the Malay word *kati*—denoting a measure of approximately 1 pound 5 ounces—was adopted into English. Early eighteenth-century boxes, called tea chests, had two or three separate compartments for different teas and sometimes also for sugar. All were lockable and the keys were guarded by the lady of the house whose responsibility it was to brew the tea for family and guests. The tea was far too precious and expensive to risk leaving in the charge of the servants, so the caddy stayed in the family drawing-room.

Caddy spoons.

English tea caddy in the style of a military chest c. 1860.

Paper filigree tea caddy.

During the late eighteenth century and through the nineteenth, chests and caddies were made from a wide variety of materials including rare woods, silver, tortoiseshell, mother-of-pearl, ivory, porcelain, and crystal. The Chinese had started producing fruit-shaped containers earlier in the eighteenth century, and English and German wooden imitations appeared as pears, apples, strawberries, eggplants, pineapples, and cantaloupes. Some were painted but most were varnished and their loose-fitting, hinged lids opened to reveal the foil-lined cavity that held the tea. As the price of tea decreased toward the end of the nineteenth century, the use of lockable caddies declined and leaves which had held pride of place in valuable ornate boxes and chests on mantle shelves and sideboards in refined drawing-rooms and private boudoirs were relegated to more cheaply produced tins and boxes that were stored in the kitchen.

The earliest caddy spoons were long-handled ladles made for use with box-like tea chests. From about 1770, short-stemmed caddy spoons began to appear, designed to fit into shorter, dumpier caddies and often in the form of a miniature scallop shell. This motif originates from the fact that oriental merchants always placed a real scallop shell in the top of tea chests to provide potential purchasers with a scoop for taking samples from the chest before deciding to buy. Spoons have been manufactured in the form of leaves, acorns, salmon, thistles, and shovels, but the most popular have always been the shell, the jockey's cap, the hand, and the eagle's wing. The "caddee shell" motif also often appears on teaspoons, tea strainers, and sugar tongs.

Bamboo strainer

English tea strainer

Swivel tea strainer

Porcelain and silver
tea strainers

STRAINERS

If using loose leaf tea, a strainer is needed for catching the leaves as the tea is poured into the cup. There are a number of strainers available on the market, the most attractive being made in silver or chrome. Plastic and stainless steel should be reserved for use in the kitchen only.

The forerunner of the modern tea strainer, which came into use in the 1790s, was the mote spoon. The pierced-bowl spoon, with its long spiky handle, appeared toward the end of the seventeenth century and was also known as a mote skimmer, long teaspoon, olive spoon, or mulberry spoon. It is possible that the spike was used to pierce olives or fruit

from a jar or lift fruit from a punch bowl, but it is more widely believed that it was intended for unblocking teapot spouts when they became clogged with swollen leaves. The spoon was used as an early caddy spoon for transferring loose leaf from caddy to pot (thus allowing any dust to fall away through the small holes), and then for skimming unwanted dust or stray leaves from the surface of the tea once it had been poured into the cup. More spoons began to disappear as strainers came into use.

The earliest strainers were made by weaving twisted wire or bamboo into a suitable shape and size. Then, like all tea wares, styles and shapes developed and changed to suit different fashions in design over the centuries.

SUGAR TONGS AND TEASPOONS

Sugar became popular in tea in Britain and the colonies by the end of the seventeenth century. In those days, sugar was available in cone-shaped blocks that had to be broken before use. Every kitchen was equipped with cast-iron pincers and little choppers for breaking pieces off when needed. For use in tea, these smaller pieces were placed in a bowl and served into the tea cups with neat silver sugar tongs. The earliest of these were made in the form of miniature coal fire andirons, changing in the 1720s and 30s to nippers shaped like small pairs of scissors. By 1770, these were phased out in favor of more practical bowl-shaped tongs.

Teaspoons developed as the taste for sugar grew, and because early tea bowls from China were small so the spoons to be used with them also had to be small. They were made as miniature tablespoons, and remained small and light until 1800 when the French influence made them larger. They then reduced again in size from about 1870. Early spoons were highly ornate, bearing scroll designs, Prince of Wales feathers, leaf patterns, emblems, mottos, political symbols, coats of arms, and crests on the back. This fashion died out in the early 1800s and, from 1850, much simpler spoons became more popular. Today, teaspoons are usually available in sets of six and are often boxed with sugar tongs for use with cubed sugar.

TEA BOWLS, CUPS, AND SAUCERS

The first tea wares used in Europe arrived from China with the early cargos of tea in the mid-seventeenth century and it was at this time that the word "china" entered the English language to denote all the dishes

New Hall teacup and saucer, c. 1800.

Coalport tea bowl.

Staffordshire teacup and saucer, c. 1835.

Oriental tea bowl, c. 1900s.

English porcelain, c. 1930s.

Teacup and saucer marked "Amherst."

Contemporary Japanese porcelain teacup and saucer.

needed for serving tea and other forms of refreshment.

Early tea bowls were handleless and tiny, holding only two or three tablespoons of tea. They were usually about 2-inches high and slightly larger in diameter. Between the 1650s and 1750s the bowl became bigger and was referred to as a "dish" of tea rather than a cup. Designs for teacup decoration were sometimes sent to China, whilst some Chinese porcelain was decorated at the English pottery. The handle was eventually adapted from the English posset cup. Chinese potters had not originally made saucers for the little bowls but these began to appear and became a standard part of tea equipage. In the eighteenth and nineteenth centuries, these were much deeper and were, in fact, used for drinking from, the hot tea being tipped into them from the cups.

THE TEA SET

As the fashion for afternoon tea grew during the nineteenth century, silversmiths, linen manufacturers, and pottery and porcelain companies began to produce a wide range of tea wares suited to the elegance of the occasion. In the eighteenth century a full tea service usually consisted of twelve tea bowls or cups and saucers, milk jug, sugar bowl, slop bowl, spoon tray, teapot, teapot stand, tea caddy or canister, hot-water jug, coffee pot, and coffee cups, and saucers. In the nineteenth century cake plates and side plates were added. Silver tea wares were made as matching sets of teapot, hot-water jug, sugar bowl, and milk jug or creamer, all of which usually sat on their own matching tray. Other equipage included teaspoons, strainers, tea knives, pastry forks, cake knives and slices, muffin dishes, tablecloths with neat matching table napkins, tray cloths, cozies, and caddies.

Traditional English tea set.

TEA
APPRECIATION

BUYING AND STORING TEA

G ROWING INTEREST IN AND DEMAND for good quality specialty teas over the past decade or so has led to an increased availability of a wider range of products. Consumers have a choice of three main sources—specialist retailers, selected major stores (some supermarkets and quality department stores), and mail-order companies. The only way to judge the quality of the products on offer is to try them. If you like the quality of what you buy, go back for more; if not, be sure to change your supplier.

SPECIALIST RETAILERS

Good retailers store loose leaf teas in large airtight caddies and sell them by weight to their customers' requirements. They may also pre-pack set quantities into caddies and packages for speed of purchase and to offer a choice of gift packs. A quality store will know what it is selling and should be able to answer your questions. You should be able to buy as much or as little as you want and, if using a store for the first time, buy only a small quantity—as little as 2 ounces if you want. Only when you are sure that the tea is to your taste should you buy in larger quantities. Even then, because tea dries out more quickly

The counter area in one of Mariage Frères' stores in Paris.

when stored in small tins, buy little and often rather than risk having larger quantities spoil at home.

Ask to see the tea before you buy. The dry leaves should have an even, pleasant appearance with particles of roughly the same size. The leaf should be glossy rather than dull and there should be no pieces of twig or stalk mixed in with the leaves. When the leaves are brewed, the infusion should be clear. Black teas should give a bright, reddish infusion; oolongs generally give an orangy-brown to dark brown brew, and the liquor from green teas should be pale yellowish-green. Good quality teas never give dull muddy liquors.

The taste should be smooth and fresh and for green teas, very light. Any tainting, mustiness, lifelessness, or strong flavors that you would not normally associate with tea usually indicate careless handling or storage, or contamination at some stage along the journey from bush to cup.

QUALITY SUPERMARKETS AND DEPARTMENT STORES

These are less likely to offer a good range of specialty teas and probably only sell teas in set quantities in pre-packed boxes, caddies, and packages. However, reputable companies should be a reliable source of good quality teas, so if you are not satisfied with your purchase, take it back, and explain the

Black tea liquor.

Oolong tea liquor.

Green tea liquor.

problem. If you find you have bought a tea that you simply do not like, do not just leave it sitting on the shelf in the storecupboard to go stale. Give it away—someone you know is bound to enjoy it.

MAIL-ORDER COMPANIES

The number of these is increasing rapidly and it is worth trying different teas from different companies until you find a supplier and a selection of teas you really like. The problem with small companies selling single-source specialty teas is that they almost certainly have to buy in bulk from the brokers or gardens, and may only sell very small quantities of each to their customers, so there is always a risk of the tea going off before it has all been sold. Be careful, order the smallest available quantity until you are sure of quality and reliability, and again, if you are not satisfied, change your supplier.

Once you have bought your tea it is important to look after it carefully. Store it in an airtight caddy (not made of glass) in a cool, dry place, away from any strong-smelling foods and other products, since tea absorbs other flavors very easily.

A list of major suppliers appears on pages 188–9.

CHOOSING WHAT TO BUY

Because there are so many different types of tea available, individual choice must depend totally on personal taste and preference. Those people who like a very light tea that is low in caffeine and has a mild taste should choose white or oolong teas; those who enjoy the aromatic herb-like refreshing qualities of green tea should buy Japanese and China green teas; drinkers of black teas will be aware of the differences between the lighter subtlety of whole leaf teas from China, the stronger darker infusions brewed from broken leaf teas and dust grades, and the robust, quick-brewing teas infused from CTC teas.

When buying tea, the purchaser needs to be aware of grading terminology (see page 39) in order to choose the best tea from a particular garden or area. For example, when choosing a Second Flush Darjeeling, Margaret's Hope FTGFOP (Finest Tippy Golden Flowery Orange Pekoe) whole leaf grade will be better quality than Margaret's Hope broken grade TGBOP (Tippy Golden Broken Orange Pekoe).

A good retailer or mail-order company should be able to explain the differences between the teas they offer and advise

Grading tea leaves in a Chinese factory.

customers according to personal preference. The customer may not always have a particularly wide choice but must assume that each company's tea buyer will have selected the best of the teas produced by a particular garden or region.

When buying tea from China, again the customer should rest assured that the tea buyer has selected the best from what is made available by the different producing provinces. If tea connoisseurs are ever fortunate enough to travel to the tea producing areas of the world, they may have the opportunity to taste teas that others have never had the chance to try.

SCENTED, FLAVORED, AND BLENDED TEAS

Flavored teas are green, oolong, or black teas that have been processed and then blended with spices or herbs, flower petals, or the essential oils of fruits. In all cases, the additional flavorings have been blended with leaves from the *Camellia sinensis* or the *Camellia assamica*, and these teas should not be confused with the wide variety of herbal or fruit infusions which contain no product of the tea plant.

Ever since they first discovered tea, the Chinese have been adding other flavorings to their tea, either by blending flowers or fruits with the processed leaf, or by adding extra ingredients to the water being boiled to brew tea, or to the brew itself.

Some Chinese teas have a natural flavor of wild orchids because the flowers grow wild among the tea bushes on the plantations. Others have the perfume of the fruit blossoms that flourish among the tea plants and open as the tea bushes are forming their new buds and leaves. All teas readily absorb other flavors (a good reason to store them carefully, away from other strong smells and flavorings), and green tea lends itself most readily to scenting.

The Chinese use three systems for naming scented teas. Either they use the name of the flower that has been added—for example Moli Huacha (Jasmine Flower Tea) and Yulan Huacha (Magnolia Flower Tea), or the name of the unflavored tea that is used for scenting is prefixed by Hua (meaning flower)—for example, Hualongjing and Hua Oolong, or thirdly, the name of the fruit used for flavoring names the tea—for example, Litchi Black (Lizhi Hongcha).

Blenders in Europe usually use the name of the fruit, flower, or spice that has been added to the raw tea—for example, Mango tea, Passion Flower tea, etc—or they give the blend a special brand name, such as Casablanca, a tea marketed by Mariage Frères in Paris which contains Moroccan mint and bergamot.

CLASSIC SCENTED TEAS
Jasmine

Jasmine tea is produced in China, mostly in the Fujian Province, and in Taiwan. This has been a favorite China tea since the days of the Song Dynasty (A.D. 960–1279). The beautifully sweet-smelling jasmine flowers are picked in the morning when they are fresh and they are kept cool during the day so that they do not open too soon. As the flowers start to open in the evening, they are piled next to the raw green, oolong, or black tea in very precise proportions. It takes about four hours for the tea to absorb the jasmine scent. For ordinary grades, the tea is spread out and then repiled for a second and third scenting. For superior grades, the spreading and piling is carried out up to seven times over a month or so. The leaves are then refired to remove any moisture in the blossoms or the tea and the blossoms are either removed or they are mixed in to give

Jasmine Pearl.

Litchi tea.

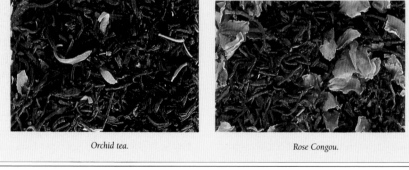

Orchid tea.

Rose Congou.

the tea an attractive appearance. Sometimes, instead of being piled beside the tea, the flowers are layered with the raw tea in tea chests, and, in some factories, the piling and mixing is done by machines.

Jasmine Monkey King has a wonderful perfume and an exquisite, subtle, and light liquor. It is a refreshing all-day or evening drink, and may be enjoyed alone, or makes a good accompaniment to spicy foods and poultry dishes.

Jasmine Pearl is a delight to look at as well as drink. Large, beautifully made pearls of pale leaf are bound with jasmine flowers. It is an excellent quality tea and has a wonderful fine flavor. It goes well with savory foods, or it may be enjoyed alone as a soothing digestif.

There are a number of other Jasmine teas that are worth trying. Look out for Jasmine Chung Feng, Jasmine Heung Pin, and Jasmine Hubei, which are all green teas. Also, try the lightly fermented Jasmine Pouchong, the semi-fermented Jasmine Mandarin Oolong, the white Jasmine Yin Hao Silver Tip, and, finally, Jasmine Yunnan, which is black.

Litchi

Lizhi Hongcha is a black tea scented with the juices from litchis, one of China's most popular fruits, which give a sharp, almost citric, flavor. It may be enjoyed alone at any time of the day or evening.

Orchid

High grade green tea from Guangdong Province is scented with the flowers of the *Chloranthus spicatus*. It produces a bright red liquor with a rich aroma. This is a refreshing and soothing drink, and is good at any time of day or night.

Rose Congou

Meigui Hongcha is a large-leafed black tea scented with rose petals. It produces a light golden liquor with a very gentle, sweet taste, and perfumed aroma. It should be served without milk to accompany light savory and sweet foods, or it may be enjoyed on its own as a refreshing and soothing drink.

Look out also for other China scented teas, including Magnolia, Chrysanthemum, and Osmanthus.

MODERN SCENTED TEAS

There are an enormous variety of these available today. Perhaps the most popular and most successful flavors are the following: black currant, cherry, citrus fruits, ginger, lemon with lemon peel, mango, minted green tea, orange with orange peel, passion flower, and red fruits.

The Japanese also produce scented teas and those recommended are Japanese Rose Sencha, and Sakura—Japanese Cherry-flavored Sencha.

CLASSIC BLENDS

All tea companies create their own blends to suit different tastes and different times of day, and there is no hard-and-fast rule as to which teas those blends include. However, there are a few classic blends that tend to contain similar mixtures of teas.

Earl Grey

Traditionally, this is a blend of China teas or China and Indian tea scented with oil from the citrus bergamot fruit—a sort of orange. The stories that explain the origin of the name vary somewhat. One tale tells how a British diplomat on a mission to·China, saved the life of a Mandarin and was given the recipe for this flavored tea as a token of thanks and as a gift to the then British Prime Minister, Earl Grey (Prime Minister from 1830–1834). Another legend says it was the Earl himself who saved the Mandarin and was given the recipe. Yet another says that the gift of tea was the conclusion to a successful diplomatic mission. However these different stories should be treated with some scepticism. First, the Chinese have

Popular flavorings for scented teas include orange, lemon, mango, mint, chrysanthemum, rose, cherry, raspberry, strawberry, and ginger.

Bergamot.

never drunk
this particular scented tea
themselves; secondly, biographies of
the Earl and numerous history books cover-
ing relations and activities involving China
and Britain between 1830 and 1834 (a time
of hostilities due to the Opium trade) make
no mention whatsoever of the gift of tea;
and thirdly, modern blends claim that the
tea should contain Indian as well as China
teas, but in 1830–34, no tea was being
produced in India so no blend could have
contained it.

The name and the stories may just have
been a clever marketing ploy by whoever
created the scented mixture. Certainly, it is
incredibly popular today and several
different types exist, using China tea,
Darjeeling, Ceylon, Silver Tip, and smoked
tea. The amount of bergamot varies, and this
makes an important difference to how good
the tea is—too much makes the infusion
taste soapy; too little, and you may as well
drink straight tea. The correct balance can
give a refreshing, lightly citrus flavor that
goes well with creamy cakes.

Yunnan Earl Grey (Roi des Earl Grey) is a
black China tea from Yunnan scented with
bergamot. It produces a beautifully balanced
flavor. It is best served without milk, and
makes a good accompaniment to fish, or
may be enjoyed at teatime.

English Breakfast

Because this is intended to accompany fatty
fried foods, such as bacon and eggs, and
strong flavors, such as smoked fish,
breakfast blends usually contain Indian
(usually Assam), Ceylon, and African teas,
although some people argue that China
Keemun is the ideal tea to drink with toast
and marmalade.

Irish Breakfast

The Irish have traditionally always liked their
tea strong and dark, and these blends consist
of rich malty Assams, sometimes with
African and Indonesian leaf added.

Afternoon Blend/Five O'Clock Tea

These are generally lighter teas blended with
Darjeelings, China, Formosa, and lighter
Ceylon teas, sometimes with a hint of added
jasmine or bergamot.

Russian Caravan

To re-create the preferred taste of the
Russians who drank China tea carried by
camel from the Russia-China border, these
blends are made up of black or oolong teas,
from China or Formosa, with a hint of smoky
Lapsang Souchong or Tarry Souchong.

HOME BLENDING

Individual preferences for tea are very personal and many drinkers blend their own mixtures at home to create a flavor they particularly like. Successful blends are the result of experimentation and tasting, trial, and error. A small amount of a good quality tea or a few leaves of a scented tea such as Jasmine or Tarry Souchong can turn an ordinary tea into something quite special.

Add perhaps a dash of Assam to Ceylon for a robust breakfast tea, a little Lapsang to Assam for a brunch or lunchtime brew, or a few leaves of Jasmine to China black for a light and refreshing afternoon blend. The possibilities are endless.

Experiment to create unusual and special blends.

TEA BAGS

The invention of the tea bag is said to have resulted from the small silk sample bags sent out to potential customers in 1908 by Thomas Sullivan, a New York City tea importer. Silk was subsequently replaced by gauze and later by paper. The market for tea bags in the U.K. began to grow in the early 1960s when approximately 5 percent of tea was brewed from bags. By 1965, the use of bags had risen to 7 percent, and by 1993, tea bags accounted for 85 percent of Britain's total consumption. In the U.S. 65–70 percent of the tea consumed is made using tea bags. World-wide, the preference is for loose leaf tea and only 16 percent of tea is made with bags.

The paper used for making tea bags is manufactured from such materials as manila hemp, wood pulp, and rayon. Modern tea-bagging machines can produce approximately 2,000 bags per minute in a variety of shapes and forms—square, round, or pyramidal, single or double chamber, heat-sealed or stapled, tagged or untagged.

TEA BAGS VERSUS LOOSE LEAF TEA

It has to be said that the quality of tea in tea bags has, in some cases, improved noticeably over the last few years, but shoppers should

U.S. company, Stash Tea, offers a wide range of bagged and loose teas.

be aware of two main types. First there is the standard everyday tea blend that is blended, packaged, and marketed in supermarkets and which, to a connoisseur, gives a poor cup of tea. But second, some producers and blenders produce bags containing good quality specialty teas and market them through major stores, in their own retail shops, or by mail-order (and sometimes by all three routes). The reason that these companies offer bags as well as loose leaf teas is because they recognize that there is a demand, even among real tea lovers, for the convenience of tea bag brewing as well as for loose leaf quality tea.

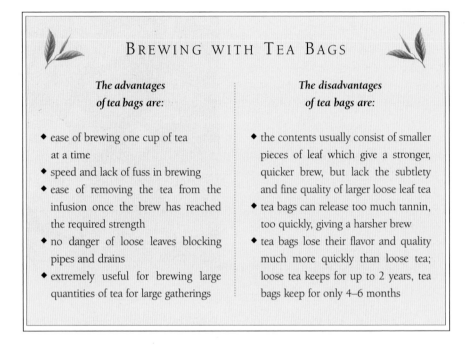

BREWING WITH TEA BAGS

**The advantages
of tea bags are:**

- ease of brewing one cup of tea at a time
- speed and lack of fuss in brewing
- ease of removing the tea from the infusion once the brew has reached the required strength
- no danger of loose leaves blocking pipes and drains
- extremely useful for brewing large quantities of tea for large gatherings

**The disadvantages
of tea bags are:**

- the contents usually consist of smaller pieces of leaf which give a stronger, quicker brew, but lack the subtlety and fine quality of larger loose leaf tea
- tea bags can release too much tannin, too quickly, giving a harsher brew
- tea bags lose their flavor and quality much more quickly than loose tea; loose tea keeps for up to 2 years, tea bags keep for only 4–6 months

Since, on the whole, tea bags give a poorer quality brew than loose leaf tea, tea bags are best relegated to emergency status in the storecupboard, for brewing on occasions when cups of tea are needed for people who do not know the difference between quality and everyday tea and where saving time is important. They are also useful for brewing large quantities for really big numbers, although this is perfectly possible with a good quality loose leaf tea brewed in a large teapot with an infuser, and decanted into suitable pots for pouring.

WATER FOR TEA

The quality of appearance and flavor of a cup of tea is affected by the water used in its preparation. The Chinese writer, Lu Yu, recommended spring water as the best. Today, most people rely on their domestic piped water supply and the quality, natural mineral content, and additional constituents such as fluoride and chlorine vary from region to region. Some tea blending companies create special blends for particular areas so that the local water will bring out the best from the leaf.

If tea is brewed using distilled, soft water or permanently hard water (containing calcium sulfate $CaSo_4$), the infusion is bright and clear. If temporary hard water (containing calcium carbonate $CaCo_3$) is used, the tea can be dull and flat and, if left to stand for only a short time, acquires a fine film of scum on the top. This is due to oxidation of tea solubles caused by the presence of the calcium and bicarbonate ions in the water. To prevent the formation of scum, avoid using temporary hard water or pass it through a water-softening filter prior to boiling.

The addition of acid to tea helps to eliminate the bicarbonate ions, so scum does not form if lemon is added. Adding sugar to tea also reduces the development of surface scum but the use of sugar is detrimental to the flavor of the tea and is not recommended. The addition of milk to tea made with hard water may help by lowering the temperature of the tea and therefore reducing the oxidation process that causes the scum, but experiments have shown that milk actually increases the amount of film on the surface, although reduced fat milks produce only half the amount of scum produced by full-fat homogenized milks.

Tea liquor should be bright and clear.

MILK IN TEA

It is impossible to know why and when the British started putting milk in their tea. It seems to have started in the days when more green tea was being consumed than black and perhaps milk helped to soften the bitter astringent flavor; or, maybe it was the result of contact by merchants with the Mongolians or the early Manchus who also put milk in their tea. Or was a little milk poured into the Chinese tea bowls used in the seventeenth and eighteenth centuries before the hot tea in order to reduce the risk of shattering the fine porcelain? Thomas Garraway's advertising broadsheet of 1660 clearly claimed that tea "being prepared with Milk and Water, strengtheneth the inward Parts," so right from the very first days of tea-drinking in Britain, milk was an option and in the mid-eighteenth century it became fashionable to take milk in tea. However, the Dutch had exactly the same contact with the same traders but did not use milk. A Dutch traveler, Jean Nieuhoff, experienced milk in tea at a banquet given by the Chinese emperor for the Dutch ambassador and his staff in 1655, but still the Dutch did not start taking milk in their tea. The French, similarly, did not show any preference for tea with milk and Marquise de la Sablière seems to have been alone in her apparent taste for it in 1680.

The custom of adding milk spread the length and breadth of Britain by the end of the seventeenth century, and subsequently traveled to the British colonies. Today, the majority of blends created for the British market are designed to be drunk with milk and producing countries bear this in mind when manufacturing teas for export to Britain. However, the addition of milk to a cup of tea is a purely personal choice, although drinkers should be aware that milk severely spoils the flavor of some teas—notably all white and green teas, pouchongs, and oolongs, most China blacks (with the exception of Yunnan), first flush Darjeelings, scented teas, and some lighter black teas.

Should the milk go into the cup before or after the tea? Tradition insists that it should go in first (as previously mentioned, originally to protect the fine porcelain tea bowls). Certainly, tea poured into milk enables the milk to mix in better. The official scientific view is that it is better to pour milk into the cup first because it then cools the first tea that is poured in, thus reducing the risk of scalding the fat in the milk—which can cause an unpleasant taste. Other people, though, prefer to add their milk afterward, claiming that it makes it easier to achieve the desired proportions of the two liquids. However, there are no hard and fast rules, it is a matter of personal preference, and no doubt the debate will run and run.

SUGAR IN TEA

The taste for sugar in tea developed in Europe towards the end of the seventeenth century and became more common in Britain than elsewhere. The custom is not thought to have come from China with the first imported teas, as the Chinese very rarely drank their tea with sugar. Only a few regions of China added sugar, the most notable being the Bohea Mountains where yellow rock sugar was stirred into the beverage.

The British liking for sweetened drinks grew so that by the late eighteenth century, consumption of sugar by the British was ten times greater than in France and other European countries. Tea spoons, spoon trays, sugar bowls, and sugar tongs became a standard part of tea equipage and the fashion traveled with emigrants to North America.

Tea specialists recommend that tea is drunk without sugar as it tends to kill the flavor of the liquor, but in Britain, many people still add one or two teaspoonfuls to a cup of tea.

BREWING A POT OF TEA

When hot water is poured on to green tea or boiling water on to oolong or black tea, the tea solubles (caffeine, tea polyphenols, and various volatile components such as essential oils) are released into the water at a rate of concentration which gradually decreases with time.

To draw out the full flavor from tea, it is essential that there is plenty of oxygen in the water being used to brew the tea. Black and oolong teas should be infused in water that has just come to a rolling boil so that it is at the correct temperature (203°F), but still holds its oxygen content. White and green teas generally prefer water at a temperature of between 158° and 203°F. For temperature recommendations, see individual tea entries in the directory.

Although there is a set of basic rules for making the perfect pot of tea, these do need to be adapted according to the type of tea and the equipment being used.

THE GOLDEN RULES

1 Use loose leaf tea that has been carefully stored and a suitable teapot. Fill the kettle with freshly drawn cold water from the faucet or filter jug and bring to a boil.

2 When the water is nearly boiling, pour a little into the teapot, swill around, and then pour away.

3 Put into the pot (or into an infuser inside the pot) 1 teaspoon tea per cup (this amount will vary according to the type of tea and personal taste).

4 Take the teapot to the boiling kettle and pour the boiling water on to the leaves. Do not allow the kettle to boil for too long. N.B. When brewing white or green tea, use water at a temperature of between 158° and 203°F, not boiling.

5 Put the lid on the pot and leave to brew for the correct number of minutes, depending on the type of leaf. If using an infuser, lift it out of the teapot as soon as the infusion has reached the desired strength. Alternatively, decant the liquor into a second warmed pot. This separates the liquid from the leaves, and avoids a bitter taste developing. For amounts of tea, water temperatures, and brewing times, see the individual recommendations in the directory.

BREWING IN A TRADITIONAL TEAPOT

To brew a pot of tea in the traditional British way, follow the Golden Rules (see page 76).

If using good quality tea, it should be possible to brew a good second pot by adding more boiling water to the leaves after the first pot has been poured. When the tea has reached its perfect strength and flavor, pour into a bone china or porcelain teacup. Some people like to warm the cup first by pouring in boiling water, leaving the cup to stand for a few minutes, then emptying before pouring the tea into the hot cup. This ensures that the tea retains its heat for as long as possible. If the liquor is brewed from leaf tea which is infused loose in the teapot, a tea strainer should be used to catch the

English bone china, c. 1840.

leaves as the tea is poured into the cup. If an infuser is used no strainer is necessary.

BREWING COMPRESSED TEA

Break off a scant 1 teaspoon of tea per cup and place in a warmed pot, an infuser in a warmed pot, or a warmed infuser mug or cup. Add boiling water and leave to infuse for about 5 minutes. Strain into a cup or tea bowl, or remove the infuser from the pot, and pour.

WHAT SORT OF TEAPOT?

For China black or green teas, a Chinese Yixing teapot is thought best to bring out the tea's full flavor, but each pot should be kept for use with only one sort of tea since the porous stoneware will acquire a lining of tea deposits which add a flavor to the tea.

Pewter, cast iron, silver, and terracotta are particularly good for strong teas such as Ceylon, African, and Assam tea. Porcelain and bone china are ideal for lighter teas such as Darjeeling, oolongs, and green teas. Ideally, you should have several pots, one for non-smoked black, one for smoked, one for flavored, and one for green tea.

Chinese Yixing stoneware teapot.

TO CLEAN
A TEAPOT

Never put a teapot into a dishwashing machine or a bowlful of soapy water. Pour away the tea, rinse with clean water, and turn upside-down to drain. Dry outside but not inside. To remove tannin from a glazed pot, or from glass or silver, fill with a solution of 2 tablespoons of baking soda and boiling water, and soak overnight. In the morning, empty, rinse thoroughly, and leave to dry.

If using a Yixing unglazed pot, never wash or clean the inside. The pot will take a little time to "settle" into its use for a particular tea, and the lining it acquires is important to the success of the brew.

DECAFFEINATED TEA

For those people who wish to avoid the intake of caffeine, decaffeinated teas are an option. It is only since the 1980s that improvements in production technology have resulted in this product being widely available. Three methods of decaffeination are used around the world and there is still some debate among scientists and decaffeinated tea manufacturers as to which is best from both health and economic viewpoints. Research is ongoing and continual advances are resulting in better quality products.

Carbon dioxide An organic solvent, it is cheap, easy to remove from the product after decaffeination, and is physiologically harmless in small quantities.

Methylene chloride This is the most popular solvent for decaffeinating both tea and coffee, is reasonably priced, and is easily removed from the product after decaffeination. A legal limit of five parts per million is placed on residual traces in the tea and the U.S. bans all imports using methylene chloride.

Ethyl acetate This is reasonably priced but is difficult to remove from the product after decaffeination. Small traces of ethyl acetate occur naturally in tea and, some say, this makes it the best solvent.

Twinings' decaffeinated tea.

INSTANT TEA

The only advantage of instant tea is that it can be made quickly. In the same way that coffee lovers would rarely even consider drinking instant coffee, so true tea connoisseurs would not dream of drinking instant tea. Since half the pleasure of tea is in the preparation, the brewing, and the enjoyment of the tea wares as well as the tea itself, to open a jar and make a cup of instant tea with a spoonful of granules is, to many people, sacrilegious. However, it is perhaps worth explaining briefly how instant tea is manufactured and how recent advances in technology are aiming to improve quality and flavor.

First, the tea leaves are infused to extract all the components that go to make a cup of tea. Leaf and liquid are then separated, the leaf discarded, and the liquid further treated to obtain a solid, dry product. This is done by three methods—evaporation of water by the application of heat, freeze concentration during which the infusion is partly frozen and ice particles are then separated, and filtering through membranes that allow the water to pass through but trap the tea solids.

The solids are then dried, either by spray-drying or by freeze-drying, and then packed into moisture-resistant packaging—usually jars—to protect the finished product on its way to the consumer.

READY-TO-DRINK (RTD) TEAS

In 1992, the American tea industry launched its first ready-to-drink (RTD) teas. The major tea companies joined up with large soft drinks manufacturers to create a range of tea-based drinks, some carbonated, some still, some with additional flavorings (such as lemon, raspberry, or peach), some containing just tea, some sweetened, others not, in bottles and in cans. These are now readily available in supermarkets and small retail stores throughout the U.S., the U.K., and Europe. Some do taste of tea, others (particularly the carbonated varieties) taste only of sugar and lemon and bear very little resemblance to the beverage that connoisseurs know and love.

In the U.S., where iced tea has always been more popular than hot tea, these trendy convenience drinks appeal to the younger consumer.

In Japan, street vending machines and supermarkets offer an even wider variety of canned ready-to-drink teas—hot or cold, green or black, with or without milk, fruit flavored or plain, sweetened or unsweetened, tea from Darjeeling or Assam—and Japanese manufacturers seem to have managed to produce a high quality product that appeals to a wide market.

ICED TEA

The idea of drinking iced tea originated at the St Louis World Trade Fair in 1904. Most of the tea drunk in the U.S. in those days was green tea from China and, in an attempt to popularize black Indian teas, a group of Indian tea producers organized a special tea pavilion staffed by Indians who offered cups of hot tea under the supervision of an Englishman by the name of Richard Blechynden. Temperatures during the fair soared and, although the British had always recognized hot tea's thirst-quenching qualities, on very hot days, the Americans totally ignored the brew and went in search of cold drinks. In a brave effort to sell his product, Blechynden packed ice cubes into glasses and poured the tea over. As word got around, customers started lining up to buy the perfect cooling beverage. So, iced tea was born and by 1992, the U.S. was consuming between 1.6 and 1.8 billion glasses of iced tea per year. More than 80 percent of all tea consumed in the U.S. is served over ice and almost 80 percent of American households drink iced tea. However, it has never caught on in Britain, and is only consumed in small amounts on extremely hot days in summer, laced with lemon and mint or borage.

To brew iced tea, choose a Ceylon or a China Keemun tea. Allow double the amount of tea normally used and brew as usual in a teapot. Strain and sweeten to taste. Fill a glass with a lot of ice and pour the hot tea over. Add a few bruised mint leaves or borage flowers and a slice of lemon or orange, then serve.

Alternatively, brew the double-strength tea, strain, sweeten, and chill in the refrigerator for several hours or overnight, then serve over ice and garnish as before.

ICED MINT TEA

Serves 4

4 sprigs fresh mint
freshly squeezed juice of 2 oranges and 4 lemons
4 cups freshly brewed strong Ceylon tea
1 small piece fresh gingerroot, shredded
2 cups cold water
sugar, to taste

Crush the mint and put it into a glass jug. Pour in the fruit juices and the strained tea. Add the ginger, sugar to taste, and the cold water. Strain and chill for at least one hour, then serve with plenty of ice, and garnish with mint leaves and a slice of orange.

Iced tea garnished with mint.

TEA AND FOOD PAIRINGS

Tea is a gourmet beverage that pairs very successfully with all types of food. Just as wines are
selected to enhance the flavor of certain foods, so teas may also be matched to particular
savory or sweet items on the menu. Different varieties of tea should be carefully chosen to
create a marriage of flavors and a truly delightful gastronomic experience.

The following is a guide to help in the choice of teas to pair with particular meals or
individual foods.

Smoked salmon pairs perfectly with Darjeeling or Lapsang Souchong.

Types of Food	Suitable Teas
Continental-style breakfast (breads, cheese, jams, etc)	Yunnan, Ceylon, Indonesian, Assam, Dooars, Terai, Travancore, Nilgiri, Kenya, Darjeeling
English-style breakfast (fried foods, eggs, smoked fish, ham, bacon, etc)	Ceylon, Kenya, African blends, Assam, Tarry Souchong, Lapsang Souchong
Light savory meals	Yunnan, Lapsang Souchong, Ceylon, Darjeeling, Assam, Green teas, Oolongs
Spicy foods	Keemun, Ceylon, Oolongs, Darjeeling, Green teas, Jasmine, Lapsang Souchong
Strong cheeses	Lapsang Souchong, Earl Grey, Green teas
Fish	Oolongs, Smoked teas, Earl Grey, Darjeeling, Green teas
Meat and game	Earl Grey, Lapsang Souchong, Kenya, Jasmine
Poultry	Lapsang Souchong, Darjeeling, Oolongs, Jasmine
Tea time	All teas
After a meal	White and green teas, Keemun, Oolongs, Darjeeling

ORGANIZING AN
AFTERNOON TEA PARTY

Afternoon tea offers the perfect occasion for relaxed conversation in an elegant and refined, yet informal, setting. It is the ideal time of day for chatting with friends or meeting new neighbors, and offering hospitality and friendship over a refreshing cup of tea. It can be very simple—with just a pot of tea and a slice of cake—or it can be an elaborate, special occasion with three courses of savory and sweet foods. In winter, settle into comfortable armchairs in the drawing-room or conservatory; in summer, take a tray or tea cart into the yard.

Invite guests by telephone, or send a simple card a couple of days before. On the day of the tea party, prepare as much as possible beforehand so that you are relaxed when your guests arrive.

Fill the kettle with freshly drawn cold water but do not boil it until you are ready to make the tea. Choose your teapot, hot-water jug, and cozy (if using). Decide which tea you are going to serve, and have the caddy ready. Set out a tea strainer, if needed, and a slop basin for taking the dregs from finished cups of tea. Place sugar or sugar cubes in a bowl with a spoon or tongs, pour milk into a jug, and prepare a dish of lemon slices.

Prepare all the food and keep covered in the refrigerator or in a cool place. You may need dishes of butter, jam, and clotted cream if scones or teabreads are to be served. Plan to serve a selection of dainty sandwiches, muffins, teabreads, scones, cakes, pastries, and cookies. These may be arranged on plates or elegant cake stands. For tea in the drawing-room, cover a side-table with a fine lace or linen cloth, or place a lace tray cloth on a tea cart. If you are planning tea in the yard, prepare a table and chairs, and cover the table with a pretty cloth.

Then prepare the following items of tea ware for each guest:

- a cup and saucer
- a teaspoon
- a side plate
- a tea knife or pastry fork, depending
on the foods to be served
- a small linen table napkin

Once you have prepared everything, change into an elegant afternoon outfit. When your guests arrive, invite them in and offer them seats. When you are sure they are comfortably settled, go to the kitchen and switch on the kettle. While it is heating up, take the food and all the things you need to the drawing-room or garden. When the kettle is boiling, make the tea.

If in the drawing-room, make sure that each guest has a small side-table on which to place their plate and cup and saucer. Hand round side plates and table napkins, giving each person a little knife or pastry fork depending on what food you are serving.

Ask each guest whether they would like milk, or lemon, or if they take their tea black. Pour each person's tea, pouring the milk, if taken, into the cup first. Take the cups of tea to each guest, and offer sugar and lemon if appropriate.

Offer foods—sandwiches first, if you are serving them. Offer more before going on to sweet items such as scones or cakes. Offer more tea as and when necessary, tipping any dregs into the slop bowl before pouring a fresh cup. Make a fresh pot of tea when necessary.

TEA AND HEALTH

Ever since tea was discovered, it has been thought to have wide-ranging health benefits and it is interesting that modern research is proving that many of the claims made over the centuries are in fact true. Tea's most obvious asset is that it is a completely natural product and contains no artificial coloring, preservatives, or flavorings (except, of course, additional flower, fruit, or spice flavorings in scented teas). It is also virtually calorie-free if taken without milk or sugar, and can play a major role in maintaining bodily fluid balance.

Since tea naturally contains fluoride, it can strengthen tooth enamel and help reduce the formation of plaque by controlling bacteria in the mouth. It thus acts as a defense against gum disease.

Animal research suggests that the consumption of both green and black tea may reduce the risk of cancer—particularly lung, colon, and skin cancer. It is thought that components in black tea may have an anti-oxidant effect, helping to prevent the formation of cancer-inducing substances in body cells.

Various research programs conducted over the last few years indicate tea's possible benefits against heart disease, stroke, and thrombosis. The reason for this is thought to

Print used to promote Japanese green tea.

be because the caffeine in tea acts as a gentle stimulant to the heart and circulatory system, and thus helps to keep the walls of the blood vessels soft, so reducing the likelihood of atherosclerosis (hardening of the arteries). It is also thought that the polyphenols in tea help to inhibit the absorption of cholesterol into the blood stream and help to prevent the formation of blood clots.

The caffeine in tea can increase concentration, alertness, and accuracy, and enhances the senses of taste and smell. It also stimulates the digestive juices and the metabolism, including the kidneys and liver, thus helping to eliminate toxins and other unwanted substances from the body.

TEA DRINKING AROUND THE WORLD

CHINA

Although China produces large quantities of black tea for export, the most popular teas in China are green and scented teas. Brewing styles vary from region to region and, in some places, teapots much like those used in the West are common. In other areas, the tea set consists of a tiny teapot (the best made of Yixing stoneware) and tiny handleless cups. The traditional way to brew a single cup of tea is by infusing leaves in a *guywan* (covered cup).

At home, tea is always offered to visitors, and in restaurants, a pot of tea is the first item brought to the table—to refresh customers before a meal—and the last—to aid digestion. In the workplace there are steaming urns of water on every floor of the factories and office blocks and tea bags in every desk ready for brewing. Workers in the fields carry gourds or jars filled with tea to refresh them throughout the day. Most of the traditional tea houses closed down in the 1920s and 30s, tea drinking being considered an "unproductive leisure activity" during the Cultural Revolution, but today the most famous of the ruined houses have been renovated and have regained much of their earlier popularity.

The Teahouse in Shanghai.

Preparing for the Japanese Tea Ceremony.

JAPAN

In Japan the preferred tea is still the traditional green leaf (particularly in the morning and as a digestif drink after a meal), and thousands of men and women attend the various tea schools to learn how to perform the Tea Ceremony. However, things are changing and many people are switching to black tea drunk with milk in the British style. The boom in black tea consumption began on a small scale about 10 years ago and has recently escalated, prompting the

opening of smart Western-style tea-rooms in hotels and shopping malls in major cities, and the development of a variety of hot and cold tea-based drinks that have fruit, fruit juices, cream, spices, or hot milk added. Tea teachers are offering seminars and classes all over Japan in order to instruct interested tea drinkers in how to brew black tea correctly and serve it in the traditional British way, accompanied by typical tea-time foods.

TIBET

Tea is considered a sacred offering in Tibet and is prepared with great care each day. To make the green salty tea, a piece of green tea brick is ground up, boiled for a few minutes in water, then the liquid is strained into a churn and mixed with goat's milk or yak butter and salt. It is called *tsampa* and is the traditional way in which tea is served in Tibet. The brew is poured into a kettle to be kept warm on the fire and then served with a flat cake made from barley or corn.

INDIA

Tea is very much the favorite drink in India, sometimes served in the British way or boiled with water, milk, and spices. Street stalls sell very strong tea with lots of sugar and milk, and on India's packed trains and train stations, tea is kept hot in large kettles and served in clay cups that are smashed and thrown away after use.

TURKEY

In Turkey, tea is far more popular than coffee, despite popular belief, and is generally brewed out of sight in the kitchen. The strong black brew is strained into little curved glasses, and served at home, in restaurants, and to business clients all day long. Some households keep a pot of tea constantly on the fire, adding fresh hot water to the leaves before serving. Tea is so important to domestic life that mothers make sure that future daughters-in-law know how to brew it correctly.

IRAN AND AFGHANISTAN

Tea is the national drink in both these countries. Green tea is drunk as a thirst quencher and black tea as a warming beverage—both taken with lots of sugar. At home and in tea houses, drinkers sit cross-legged on mats on the floor and sip their tea from brightly colored porcelain pots.

RUSSIA

Russians started drinking tea in the seventeenth century, but the beverage did not become widely popular until the beginning of the nineteenth century. In Russia, both green and black tea are drunk without milk from glasses that often have a metal handle. A lump of sugar or a spoonful of jam is taken into the mouth before the tea is sipped. The samovar, still very much part

Russian samovar.

of Russian household equipment today, became popular in the 1730s and seems to have developed from a firepot used by the Mongolians. The samovar's metal container has a fire underneath and a pipe that runs up the middle to keep the water hot. Very strong tea is brewed in the little teapot that sits on the top and this is diluted with hot water drawn from a tap on the side of the samovar. The samovar keeps tea hot for hours and provides a ready supply for any number of household members or guests.

EGYPT

The Egyptians are avid tea drinkers and like the beverage strong and sweet without milk. In cafes it is served in glasses that sit on a tray which also holds a glass of water, sugar, a spoon, and sometimes mint leaves.

MOROCCO

Tea is served in glasses on silver trays. It is the man's job in Moroccan households to pour the tea and he holds the long-spouted pot high above the glass as he pours, so that each glass of tea has a slightly frothy head to it. It is often served with candies.

Tea server in Morocco.

NEW ZEALAND AND AUSTRALIA

In both these countries, tea is served at home and in restaurants in the British fashion but the Australian bushman makes his own unique brew in a billycan.

As in Britain and other European countries, the increased consumption of coffee and soft drinks has gradually caused a reduction in tea consumption. In Australia, imports of tea reached a high of 40,785.4 tons in 1967 but since then they have declined to a steady 23,148.5 tons per year—approximately 28 pounds 8 ounces per person.

THE U.K.

Tea is still Britain's favorite beverage, despite competition from coffee and soft drinks, although consumption is declining very slightly. The average Briton drinks approximately 3.32 cups of tea a day—down from 3.88 cups in 1984. Some people start each day with at least one cup of tea and drink tea at work—in morning and afternoon breaks and sometimes at lunchtime; and afternoon tea is still an essential part of British life. Few people drink tea in the evenings and the U.K. Tea Council recently launched a promotional program with the catering trade in order to encourage restaurants to offer tea as a healthy alternative to coffee after meals.

Since the early 1980s, there has been a new surge of interest in the 'ceremony' of Afternoon Tea, and tea shops, tea rooms, and hotel tea lounges are thriving. Foreign visitors and Britons alike are enjoying the elegance and style of tea and teatime.

Yet, in many British homes, tea is brewed with tea bags which give a brew that, to connoisseurs, has little taste. However, there are still plenty of people in Britain who know how to brew and serve an excellent cup of tea and, even though consumption is down, there is a growing awareness of the many different sorts of quality tea. One company that has made specialty teas more readily available is Whittard of Chelsea who have opened retail stores in all major shopping malls and main streets. As well as an excellent range of single source and blended teas, the stores sell a colorful selection of tea

wares and gift packs. Twinings' original store at 216 Strand, London, dates back to 1706 and continues to delight visitors with its range of teas, tea wares, and tea books and, on the walls, portraits of past members of the Twinings family.

For many people in Britain, it is still tea that they turn to when there are problems to be solved, sympathy to be offered, when the day has been too long or the work too hard, when the winter cold is too severe, or the summer heat too exhausting. Nothing else will do—it has to be a cup of tea!

THE U.S.

Although the U.S. is generally thought of as a coffee-drinking nation, a revolution in tea drinking started about 10 years ago, coincing with a revival of interest in the U.K. The reasons may be a wider concern

Selection of products from U.S. tea company, Grace Rare Teas.

The Rotunda tea-room at New York's Pierre Hotel on Fifth Avenue and 61st Street.

with health and a fascination with the nostalgic qualities associated with tea drinking. Today, more than 125 million Americans drink tea daily in one form or another—hot black tea, iced tea, or ready-to-drink bottled or canned tea.

The specialty tea market is growing, and more and more energetic and enthusiastic people are opening tea-rooms, or adding tea outlets to existing businesses such as gift stores. Tea specialists are offering presen-tations, demonstrations, and promotional and celebratory tea events, training their customers to brew tea properly. A growing number of mail-order companies are offering rare and exclusive teas that have been carefully selected from quality sources. As well as a wide variety of teas, the mail-order catalogs and internet listings also include unusual tea wares such as Yixing teapots, Japanese tea sets, and *guywans*, as well as tea-time foods to serve with afternoon tea.

GLOBAL

TEA

DIRECTORY

TEA-PRODUCING
COUNTRIES OF THE
WORLD

THE AZORES

ECUADOR

PERU

BRAZIL

ARGENTINA

CAM

R

BU.

ZIM.

C.I.S

TURKEY

IRAN

NEPAL

CHINA

JAPAN

TAIWAN

INDIA

ANDA

ETHIOPIA

BANGLADESH

VIETNAM

MALAYSIA

KENYA

SRI LANKA

INDONESIA

PAPUA NEW GUINEA

TANZANIA

MALAWI

MAURITIUS

MOZAMBIQUE

MADAGASCAR

SOUTH FRICA

AUSTRALIA

KEY

DETAILED DIRECTORY ENTRY

OTHER TEA-PRODUCING COUNTRIES

A GUIDE TO THE TEAS OF THE WORLD

AFRICA

CAMEROON

Three estates produce three very different teas—one clonal, one high-grown, and one low-grown—all of very good quality.

KENYA

CTC teas grown here are normally sold as Kenya blends or for blending with teas from other producing areas. Teas give rich, dark brews with body and full flavor.

MALAWI

CTC teas mostly sold for blending. Recent improvements in quality are due to clonal replanting, but drought over the past few years has badly affected the region.

SOUTH AFRICA

Produces black teas, most of which are consumed by the home market, but "Zulu" tea, the only South African tea

currently marketed abroad, is becoming very popular in Europe and the U.S.

TANZANIA

Produces CTC and orthodox teas, similar in character to Ceylon teas; although quality varies according to altitude and plucking standards. Problems of drought and acute shortage of labor have recently affected the quality of the teas.

INDIAN SUB-CONTINENT

INDIA

Assam

Full-bodied, malty, rich-flavored orthodox teas, with strength and color are grown in this area.

Darjeeling

Teas from different times of the year have distinctly different flavors—First Flush is a greenish leaf that gives an astringent perfumed tea, Second Flush gives a gentler, more rounded flavor; In-Betweens combine the astringency of first flush with the more mature flavor of second flush; and Autumnals give a tea with a rounded flavor.

Dooars

This small region, to the west of Assam, produces low-grown teas with body and strength.

Nilgiri

The teas grown on the range of Nilgiri Hills in the south of India give a flavory brisk liquor with a mellow taste.

Sikkim

This tiny Indian state produces Darjeeling-type teas, but with more body and flavor.

Terai

A small area south of Darjeeling grows teas that give a rich colored brew and a spicy taste.

Travancore

This southern region produces teas with similar characteristics to Ceylon teas—rich color and full-bodied.

SRI LANKA

Six different regions produce teas with individual characteristics. High-grown teas give very fine quality light golden liquors; middle-grown give rich, coppery red teas; low-grown give dark, strong teas usually used in blends. Nuwara Eliya, the highest area, produces the finest of Sri Lanka's teas.

THE FAR EAST

CHINA
Seventeen provinces produce the widest range in the world of excellent quality white, green, oolong, pouchong, black, compressed, and scented teas, many still made by hand.

INDONESIA
Most teas are sold for blending. They give a bright, light, slightly sweet infusion, a little like high-grown Ceylons.

JAPAN
Produces only green teas. Gyokura, Sencha, and Houjicha are fine needle-leaf teas that are infused in water; Tencha is cut into fine pieces, and Matcha is powdered and whisked into water, producing a frothy liquor.

TAIWAN
Produces green, oolong, and black orthodox teas. Oolongs are the specialty of Taiwan. Fermented slightly longer than China oolongs and therefore blacker and slightly stronger. Lightly fermented pouchongs are also manufactured.

OTHER TEA-PRODUCING COUNTRIES

SOUTH AMERICA
ARGENTINA
Black tea used mainly for blending in China and the U.S.

BRAZIL
Black teas that give a bright infusion. Mostly used in blends.

ECUADOR
Produce black teas, mainly exported to the U.S.

PERU
Black teas grown on two estates.

AFRICA
BURUNDI
Black CTC teas.

ETHIOPIA
Good quality teas produced in two factories.

MADAGASCAR
Clonal teas with an attractive quality, of East African standard.

MAURITIUS
Orthodox black teas.

MOZAMBIQUE
Strong, black spicy teas.

RWANDA
Black CTC teas of good quality., but unpredictable because of political instability.

UGANDA
Black teas, used in blending.

ZIMBABWE
Black teas that give strong dark liquor similar to Malawi teas.

EUROPE
AZORES
Black teas are grown on rehabilitated plantations.

ASIA
BANGLADESH
Produces black teas, mostly used in blending.

C.I.S.
CTC and orthodox teas.

IRAN
Smallholder growers produce light flavored black teas.

MALAYSIA
Poor quality teas, sold mainly to the tourist trade.

NEPAL
Darjeeling-type black teas.

TURKEY
Black teas, mostly for the domestic market.

VIETNAM
Black CTC and green teas.

OCEANIA
AUSTRALIA
Black teas for domestic market.

PAPUA NEW GUINEA
Black tea with dark liquor and strong taste.

HOW TO USE THIS BOOK

This guide is split into four main sections. The first three sections look in detail at 11 of the world's tea-producing nations. These have been given precedence because of the quantity of tea they produce, the excellent quality of their teas, or they are producing teas that are of particular interest to the connoisseur and they have optimism for the future. The last section of the directory looks briefly at other tea-producing countries of the world and where possible, a tea garden has been recommended.

For each country of origin in the first three sections of the directory, specific teas are recommended as being the very best or examples of the very best. In some areas, there are so many excellent teas from individual gardens that it would be impossible to list them all.

In recommending teas from specific gardens, it is only possible to give general characteristics, since each tea can vary from year to year according to annual variations in weather patterns and local conditions.

The entry for each tea gives brewing instructions and recommendations as to how and when to drink the particular tea. These are guidelines only.

The amounts of tea brewed and the length of the infusion may vary according to personal preference for the strength of each brew. Individual taste will also differ as to when and how the teas are drunk, and with which foods, if any, they are paired.

A scant 1 cup measure is approximately the amount of water needed for one cup of tea. Multiply the amount of water and tea according to how many cups are to be brewed. Each cup of tea will require approximately 1 teaspoonful of loose leaf tea, although this varies slightly according to the size of leaf used.

Drinking recommendations
Key to symbols

| Breakfast | Morning | Afternoon | All day (can be drunk for breakfast through to early evening) | Digestif | Evening | Bedtime | Special Occasions |

AFRICA

CAMEROON

*Interesting teas for connoisseurs who are looking
for something a little eccentric.*

Between 1884 and 1914, German planters cultivated numerous crops which included coffee, oil palm, tobacco, kole nuts, and bananas, and they also experimented with growing tea. The first tea bushes were planted in 1914 at Tole on the fertile slopes of Mount Cameroon—West Africa's only active volcano in the southwest of the country, overlooking Limbe on the Atlantic coast.

Tole is situated at an elevation of 2,000 feet above sea-level, and conditions for tea are good. Annual rainfall is about 120 inches, temperatures range from 66° to 82°F, and humidity is high. The tea plantations cover 66 acres. Although the initial

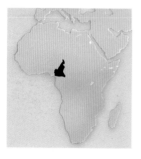

Tole Factory set against Mount Cameroon.

plantings were developed during the 1940s and tea production expanded, the operation was discontinued in 1948 and did not start again until 1952, when several plots of tea were rehabilitated. In 1954, it was decided to develop Tole as a 700-acre estate and by 1968, about 795 acres had been planted, and production of orthodox black teas had reached 685.6 tons annually.

Further tea plantations were developed at Ndu in the steep grasslands of the northwest province. Using seed from Tole and from East Africa, the new plantations were set out in 1957 at an elevation of 7,000 feet, and an orthodox processing factory was built. Thus, by 1968, Cameroon had two tea estates comprising of 1,823 acres of tea.

Ndu

Characteristics
High-grown orthodox black tea, grown at 7,000 feet. Bright colory liquor.

Brewing hints
Brew 1 teaspoon in a scant 1 cup water at 203°F. Infuse for 2 minutes.

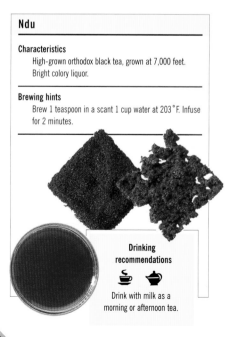

Drinking recommendations

Drink with milk as a morning or afternoon tea.

Djuttitsa Clonal

Characteristics
Good quality, high-grown clonal CTC tea, grown at 5,500 feet. Bright liquor with good flavor.

Brewing hints
Brew 1 teaspoon in a scant 1 cup water at 203°F. Infuse for 3 minutes.

Drinking recommendations

Drink with milk as a morning or afternoon tea.

Tole

Characteristics
Interesting low-grown CTC leaf that gives good, bright color, and medium quality flavor.

Brewing hints
Brew 1 teaspoon in a scant 1 cup water at 203°F. Infuse for 3 minutes.

Drinking recommendations

Good at any time of day with a little milk.

Today, the total area under tea is about 3,890 acres, of which 1,482 acres are planted with cloned tea bushes. The leaf is plucked throughout the year and during the peak season a workforce of 2,300 men and women are employed to harvest the tea. Annual production is 4,067.5 tons and this is expected to increase to 4,629.7 by the year 2000.

In the 1950s, all Cameroon tea was sold at the London auctions. Until 1965, 60 percent was exported to Europe and Nigeria, but since 1966, a higher proportion has been sold locally. Today, the republics of Chad and Sudan are Cameroon's principal markets. However, modernization of factories, and development and extension of planted areas is continuing, and the introduction of CTC processing is expected to increase offerings to the London auctions.

Cameroon tea is extremely interesting for connoisseurs who are looking for something a little eccentric. The three factories within this small country produce three very different teas. Tole's low-grown teas, Ndu's high-grown teas, and Djuttitsa's clonal teas are all of excellent quality.

KENYA

Quality teas grown in the lush Kenya Highlands.

THE FIRST TEA BUSHES WERE PLANTED at Limuru in Kenya in 1903 and production increased slowly in the highlands of Kericho and Nandi until the late 1950s when smallholders started growing tea on a trial basis. In 1950, it had been recognized that tea was a very important commodity for the country and the Tea Board of Kenya was established to regulate the industry. The Kenya Tea Development Authority was founded in 1964 with the objective of promoting the development of tea cultivation by Kenyan smallholders in suitable areas of the country. A total of 19,775 smallholder growers in 1964 on 10,905 acres of land has increased to present figures of 269,839 growers on 222,395 acres.

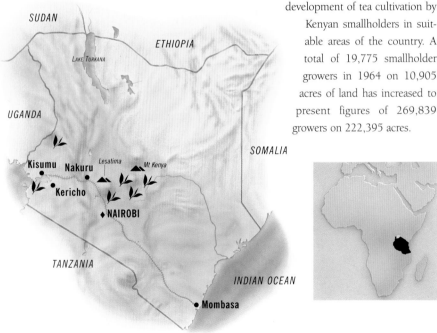

In the 1960s, there was only one factory, Ragati in Nyeri, but 43 more have been established in 13 tea-growing districts, and these handle a total of 27,557.8–33,069.3 tons of green leaf every year. The black CTC teas produced are very tippy and give a strong, rich, full-bodied liquor with an almost sweet fragrance. They are widely used in blending. One garden, Marinyn, produces a high quality, orthodox leaf that looks rather like an orthodox Assam.

The main growing areas are in the Kenya Highlands—an area ranging in altitude from 5,000 to 9,000 feet and where plenty of rainfall helps the bushes to produce quality leaf. Whereas most of Kenya is too dry to support arable crops, the mountains benefit from the warm, moist air that rises from Lake Victoria and turns to rain above the higher ground. The bushes flush all year, but the best teas are harvested in late January/early February and July. The quality of the teas is

Kenyan tea pickers at work.

so consistently high that the industry has become one of the world's major producers. In 1992, Kenya ranked third after China and India, with a production of 207,234.3 tons–7.8 percent of world production. Exports during that year were 182,983.5 tons, 16.5 percent of total world exports. In 1993, an all-time high was recorded of 232,587.4 tons, 207,234.3 tons of which were exported. The teas fetch premium prices on world markets. Traditional outlets have been the Mombasa auctions, the London auctions, and direct sales overseas and to domestic buyers. Major foreign customers include the U.K., Ireland, Germany, Canada, The Netherlands, Pakistan, Japan, Egypt, and Sudan.

Kenya Blend

Characteristics
Good balanced flavor from golden red rich liquor.

Brewing hints
Brew 1 teaspoon in a scant 1 cup water at 203°F. Infuse for 2-3 minutes.

Drinking recommendations

Drink with milk as a breakfast or afternoon tea. Excellent with chocolate cakes and desserts.

Marinyn

Characteristics
Beautiful orthodox leaf with plenty of tip from Kenya's most famous garden. Gives a strong rich infusion with body and a full fruity flavor.

Brewing hints
Use 1 teaspoon in a scant 1 cup water at 203°F. Infuse for 2-3 minutes.

Drinking recommendations

Drink with milk as an afternoon tea.

MALAWI

A recent program of clonal replanting has led to an improvement in quality.

MALAWI IS AFRICA'S SECOND MOST IMPORTANT tea producer after Kenya. The first tea was introduced, to what was then Nyasaland, as seed from the Royal Botanic Gardens, Edinburgh, Scotland, in 1878. Around the turn of the century, plantations were laid out at Lauderdale, Thornswood, and Thyolo with seed from Natal which had come originally from Ceylon.

TANZANIA

ZAMBIA

Nkhata Bay

LAKE NYASA

MOZAMBIQUE

LILONGWE

LAKE MALOMBE

LAKE CHIUTA

LAKE CHILWA

Blantyre

Mt Mulanje

Mulanje

The first tea was exported in 1905, and although the early production was not of particularly good quality, the industry thrived and, by the mid-1950s, more than 12,355 acres had been planted. Most of the tea areas are situated at low altitudes—the average in Mulanje district being just 1,800 feet above sea-level—and the unpredictable rainfall patterns and high temperatures are not ideal for tea. In 1966, the Tea Research Foundation (Central Africa) was established, essentially because of the distinct environment in which tea is grown in this region. In 1992, severe drought and uneven rainfall distribution following low rainfall in 1990 and 1991, badly affected the tea crop. Even

A breeding selection plot at the Mimosa Tea Research Foundation.

in the best years planters can never be sure what the weather will do. They always hope that dry conditions will not adversely affect the bushes, but in 1992, with the low rainfall and above-normal temperatures, new plants shrivelled and died, the flush was mediocre, and established bushes suffered long-term damage. By 1994, however, crops had recovered and average annual production is 44,092.4 tons.

Most Malawi teas are used as "filler" teas in blending, but a recent program of clonal tea breeding and replanting has led to an improvement in quality and an increase in prices at the London auction.

Namingomba

Characteristics
Good quality, pure clonal tea. Bright liquor with good color and full-bodied flavor.

Brewing hints
Brew 1 teaspoon in a scant 1 cup water at 203°F. Infuse for 3 minutes.

Drinking recommendations

Drink with milk at all times of the day, especially in the morning.

Kavuzi

Characteristics
Small leaf LTP (similar to CTC) tea produced in the north of Malawi. Gives strong full-colored tea.

Brewing hints
Brew 1 teaspoon in a scant 1 cup water at 203°F. Infuse for 3 minutes.

Drinking recommendations

A good breakfast tea, drink with milk.

SOUTH AFRICA

Zulu tea has found a niche market in Europe and the U.S.

T HE FIRST TEA PLANTS IN SOUTH AFRICA, brought from Kew Gardens in England, were planted south of the Limpopo River in the Durban Botanical Gardens, Natal, in 1850. When commercial cultivation started in 1877, the seeds planted were from Assam. By 1881/82, production had reached just over ¼ ton and by 1884/85, had increased to 28.5 tons. In 1886, Natal produced 40 tons—all for local consumption—and in 1889, there were some dozen estates with 1,090 acres under tea.

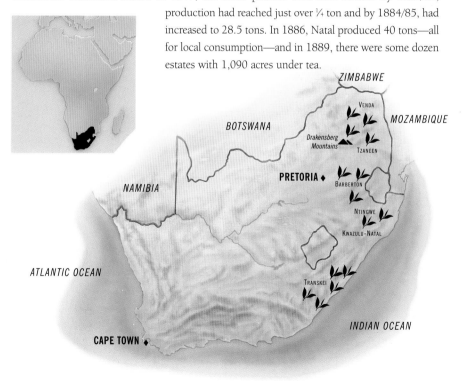

Packing tea in a South African tea factory.

In the early part of this century, commercial cultivation started in KwaZulu-Natal, but by 1949, production had ceased due to high labor and packaging costs, and depressed world markets. In the 1960s, the tea-producing company, Sapekoe, was established, and new areas for production were planted along the Drakensberg mountains in Eastern Transvaal and in parts of Natal and the Transkei. Since 1973, more estates have been set up in the Levubu area, in Venda, and in central Zululand near Ntingwe.

Plucking tea during the harvesting season.

South Africa is also famous for its Rooibosch (Rositea) or red tea which is processed from the leaf of *Aspalathus linoaris*, not from *Camellia sinensis*. The liquor, which looks and tastes much like tea and is drunk with milk in the same way, is becoming well known throughout Europe and the U.S. Its popularity is probably due to the fact that it is 100 percent caffeine free and is rich in vitamin C, mineral salts, and proteins.

The leaf is harvested in the short rainy season from November to March and most is processed by a modified CTC method. In the early 1990s, drought conditions had an adverse effect on both production and quality, but tea bushes recover remarkably well and the South African industry is optimistic about both production and increased domestic consumption.

South Africans drink approximately 10 billion cups of tea annually—about 67 percent of which is in tea bags. Because of such high consumption within the country, almost all of the teas grown are sold locally and are very rarely seen in the world auctions. However, Zulu tea is currently being exported from the Ntingwe Tea Estate in KwaZulu-Natal and has found a niche market in northern England, marketed by Taylors of Harrogate in the company's "Betty's" tea-shops, and is popular elsewhere in Europe and the U.S.

Zulu Tea

Characteristics
Clonal black tea that gives a fresh, lively brew.

Brewing hints
Brew 1 teaspoon in a scant 1 cup water at 203° F. Infuse for 2-3 minutes.

Drinking recommendations

☽🍴

Drink with milk. Perfect breakfast tea.

T A N Z A N I A

Quality of tea varies according to the altitude and plucking standards.

G ERMAN SETTLERS WERE THE FIRST TO grow tea at Amari and Rungwa in Tanzania in about 1905, but commercial production did not start until 1926. A factory was opened at Mufindi in 1930 and the industry expanded slowly and steadily in the Southern Highlands and the Usambaras. Today, the main producing areas are Rungwa, Mufindi, Njombe, Usambara, and Kagera. The total area under cultivation is approximately 49,421 acres, about 50 percent of which is owned by private producers and the rest by smallholders. Smallholder tea production

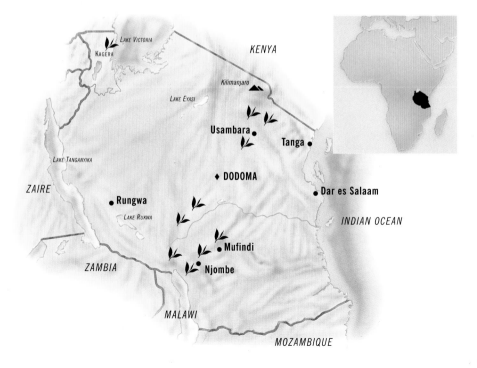

began in 1961 after independence, and today grows approximately 30 percent of the total green leaf supply. The industry operates on two levels: private estates grow and manufacture their own tea; the Tanzania Tea Authority (TTA) buys green leaf from smallholders and processes it at TTA factories. Currently, the private sector owns 14 factories, the TTA owns five, and two more are joint private/TTA ventures.

Production tends to vary from year to year due to such problems as lack of transport to carry the green leaf to the factories, a shortage of labor at peak plucking times, a shortage of fuel, the need for refurbishment of the factories, drought, etc. However, production has gone up over the past eight years, and increased investment and more attractive financial deals for tea exports have led to a more stable outlook and expectations of improved quality and increased production.

About 70 percent of Tanzania's tea is exported and the remaining 30 percent is consumed locally. The quality of the tea varies according to the altitude and plucking standards. Some factories produce very good quality CTC BP1, PF1, and PDust grades, and average prices tend to be higher than for Malawi, Uganda, and Zimbabwe teas.

Kilima

Characteristics
Excellent black tea grown at 6,000–7,000 feet. Similar character to a Ceylon tea. Gives a strong, fruity infusion.

Brewing hints
Brew 1 teaspoon in a scant 1 cup water at 203°F. Infuse for 2-3 minutes.

Drinking recommendations

Drink with a little milk as a breakfast or afternoon tea.

Preparing cuttings for the nursery.

INDIAN
SUB-CONTINENT

INDIA

One of the world's largest producers of tea, with more than 13,000 gardens.

A DUTCH EXPLORER WHO SAILED ROUND the Cape of Good Hope to Goa on India's west coast in the late sixteenth century, mentioned the tea-drinking customs of the Indian people. In his book, *Voyages and Travels of Jan Huyghen van Linschoten*, published in 1598, he tells how the leaves of the Assam tree were used by the Indians both as a vegetable, eaten with garlic and oil, and as a drink.

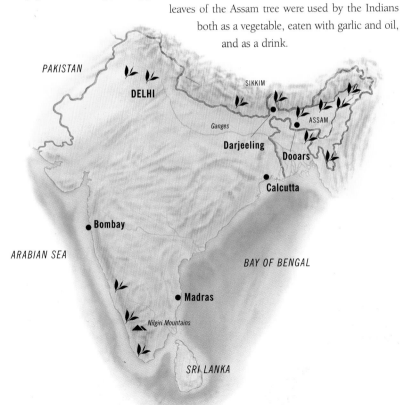

PAKISTAN

DELHI

SIKKIM

Ganges

Darjeeling

ASSAM

Dooars

Calcutta

Bombay

ARABIAN SEA

BAY OF BENGAL

Madras

Nilgiri Mountains

SRI LANKA

In 1784, the British botanist, Sir Joseph Banks, declared that the Indian climate was favorable to tea cultivation, but did not know that the plant already grew there. In 1823, Robert Bruce, a Scottish mercenary, came across the native Indians drinking tea made with a different variety of the plant than the one already known in China. He and his brother Charles, who worked for the British East India Company, arranged for some of the indigenous plants to be cultivated in the botanical gardens of Calcutta. Despite a determination on the part of the East India Company that only Chinese plants were good enough for commercial production, the Bruce brothers managed, in 1835, to convince them that the *Camellia assamica* would thrive where the *Camellia sinensis* would not. Plantations were established, and the first consignment of eight chests of Assam teas arrived in London in 1838. However the new operation did not become profitable until 1852. Claims were made that the new plantations would create opportunities for work and that the local Indians would therefore benefit but, in fact, the early estates used mainly imported Chinese labor. The Assam Tea Company was established in 1840 and soon expanded its activities into other north Indian areas. Production steadily increased and exports rose from 183.4 tons in 1853 to 6,700 tons in 1870. In 1885, production was 35,274

tons (of which 34,171.7 tons were exported) and by 1947, when India won its independence from Britain, production had reached 281,089.6 tons.

Today, India is one of the world's largest producers of tea. With more than 13,000 gardens and a total workforce of more than two million people, India produces approximately 30 percent of the world's black teas and 65 percent of CTC teas. The change from orthodox to CTC manufacture in many of the Indian factories was the result of a growing British and Irish market and the developing preference, from the 1950s onward, for a quick-brewing strong tea bag tea.

Indian gardens follow different methods of production depending on the markets they are catering for. Some concentrate on the CTC production of fannings and dust for the export market. Some make mainly CTC granular broken grades and fannings for the domestic market, and others manufacture orthodox tippy whole leaf grades for the specialty market.

In 1993, 587,532.4 tons of CTC teas were produced (compared to 544,542.2 tons in 1992)—almost 83 percent of production— and the manufacture of orthodox teas has reduced slightly in recent years. India's home market has been steadily growing over the past 45 years. In 1951, domestic demand was for only 80,468.8 tons (approximately 30 percent of production). By 1991, that

A top quality clone of the Nilgiris.

Shear plucking in a Nilgiri tea plantation.

had risen to 573,202.4 tons (approximately 75 percent of production). But the Indian planters have always managed to meet their export commitments and the Tea Board of India, with all its affiliated research bodies in all the major tea-growing areas of north and south India, follow a carefully formulated long-term strategy for increased production and productivity.

One aspect of this program has been established in order to protect the reputation of India's three main specialty teas—Darjeeling, Assam, and Nilgiri. As the world-wide reputation for these teas has grown over the years, and international demand has increased, a situation arose whereby traders were offering tea misleadingly labeled as Pure Darjeeling, Pure Assam, and Pure Nilgiri, but which were, in fact, mixed with teas from other areas. Therefore, it became necessary to ensure the quality of these teas worldwide. The Tea Board of India has now introduced three distinctive logos as a guarantee that packets contain 100 percent

Logos of specialty teas.

Darjeeling, Assam, or Nilgiri and that those teas have been bought from companies that are checked and certified by the Tea Board. The Darjeeling logo shows the profile of a female Indian plucker holding a tea shoot of two leaves and a bud, the Assam logo bears the image of the one-horned rhino that lives in Assam's Brahmaputra Valley; and the Nilgiri logo depicts the undulating hills of the Blue Mountains (Nilgiris) of Southern India. These symbols help the consumer to identify the genuine quality of India's three specialty teas.

The pattern of India's exports has changed markedly since 1947. In that year, the major buyer was the U.K. (140,214.1 tons—66.3 percent of exports) and very small amounts were purchased by areas such as Eastern Europe and the various Arab states. Today, India's major customers are in Iran, Poland, Egypt, and the former U.S.S.R., while Britain's purchases have dropped to 15.7 percent of total exports. Japan is a newcomer, and shows a preference for Darjeelings, tippy orthodox teas, and Nilgiris.

Although India produces mostly black teas, a small amount of green tea is produced, mainly for the Afghanistan market, in the Kangra Valley, north of Delhi. India also has several organic plantations, notably Mullootor and Makaibari in Darjeeling, which operate a system of chemical-free agriculture and environmental conservation.

ASSAM

Today, tea is grown on both sides of the Brahmaputra Valley, the largest black tea-producing region of the world. In 1993, approximately 155 years after those first chests of tea arrived in London, Assam's 2,000 gardens produced a record 444,231.8 tons—53 percent of the all-India record crop of 835,552.7 tons.

The Brahmaputra Valley lies 120 miles east of Darjeeling, and borders with China, Burma, and Bangladesh. The tea-growing areas experience very high rainfall—from 79 to 118 inches per year. The rainfall distribution is extremely uneven and can be as high as 10–12 inches per day in the monsoon period. During this time of heavy rains, the temperature rises to approximately 203°F and this greenhouse-like combination of humidity and heat produces some of the finest varieties of tea in the world.

The majority of Assam production takes place from July to September when nearly 1,000 pluckers work eight hours a day in the hot steamy gardens, each one picking nearly 50,000 stems a day. Conditions are not easy and apart from the intense heat, snakes and insects make life very uncomfortable. The leaves are thrown into heavy baskets that are worn on the back and supported by a strap around the forehead.

To meet an increasing domestic demand and to keep up a steady export trade, the Assam industry has concentrated over the past few years on the breeding and selection of superior clone plants and seed stock, and bio-technical research into plant improvement. To ease the shortage of labor during peak

Young tea in a drainage improvement project in Assam.

seasons, mechanical plucking has also been tested in some areas.

Manufactured CTC and orthodox teas are transported by truck to the nearest auction centers at Guwuhati (which handles mainly teas for the domestic market), Silgiri, and Calcutta (which auctions teas for export).

FIRST FLUSH ASSAM

Assam tea bushes start growing after their winter dormancy in March and the first flush is picked for eight to ten weeks. First flush Assams, unlike Darjeelings, are seldom marketed in Europe and the U.S.

SECOND FLUSH ASSAM

The plucking of the second flush begins in June and the major part of production takes place from July to September. The undersides of the large leaves of the *Camellia assamica* are covered with an abundance of silvery hairs and give high quality tippy teas. When brewed, they yield a rich aroma, a clear dark red liquor that is full of body, and a strong, malty rounded taste that is a favorite at breakfast time.

Bamonpookri

Characteristics
Regular-size, well-made pieces of greeny-brown leaf similar to first flush Darjeeling. Excellent quality tea with a strong fresh flavor.

Brewing hints
Brew 1 teaspoon in a scant 1 cup water at 203°F. Infuse for 3 minutes.

Drinking recommendations

)ᵀᵀ

A breakfast tea. Drink with a little milk.

Napuk

Characteristics
Balanced flavor, wonderful aroma, and all the qualities of well-made Assam tea.

Brewing hints
Brew 1 teaspoon in a scant 1 cup water at 203°F. Infuse for 3–4 minutes.

Drinking recommendations

)ᵀᵀ

Drink with milk. Very good at breakfast time with toast and marmalade.

Thowra

Characteristics
Beautifully made leaves with plenty of golden tips.
Strong, spicy liquor with lots of body.

Brewing hints
Brew 1 teaspoon in a scant 1 cup
water at 203°F. Infuse for 3–4
minutes.

**Drinking
recommendations**

An excellent breakfast tea.
Best with milk.

ASSAM BLEND

The malty, full-bodied richness of Assam blends makes them ideal morning teas that drink extremely well with breakfast foods such as bacon, ham, and smoked fish.

Assam Blend

Characteristics
Pungent, malty, full-bodied liquor with rich red color.

Brewing hints
Brew 1 teaspoon in a scant 1 cup water at 203°F. Infuse
for 3–4 minutes.

**Drinking
recommendations**

Drink with milk as a strong
breakfast or afternoon tea.

Other recommended gardens

Betjan, Bhuyanphir, Borengajuli, Dinjoye, Hajua, Halmari, Harmutty, Jamirah, Maud, Meleng, Nokhroy, Numalighur, Sankar, Seajuli, Sepon, Silonibari and Tara.

ASSAM GREEN

Green tea accounts for slightly more than 1 percent of India's total tea production. Assam produces very little of this type of tea, but the unusual light, almost sweet liquor is worth trying.

Khongea

Characteristics

An Assam green tea. Young leaves give a scented aroma and a clear, golden liquor with a sweet flavor.

Brewing hints

Brew 2 teaspoons in a scant 1 cup water at 194–203°F. Infuse for 2½ minutes.

Drinking recommendations

A relaxing tea at any time of the day. Drink without milk.

DARJEELING

Tucked away in the foothills of the snow-covered Himalayan mountains of northeast India lies the hill resort of Darjeeling 6,000 feet above sea-level and in the most spectacular setting, surrounded by over 49,421 acres of tea bushes. On a clear day, Mount Everest is visible in the distance. Good Darjeelings are always referred to as the "Champagne" of teas, the subtle, muscatel flavor and wonderful aroma being produced by the unique combination of cool, misty climate, elevation, rainfall, terrain, and the quality of the soil and air.

Most of the bushes cultivated in the Darjeeling region are grown from China seed, China hybrid, or hybrid Assam bushes. The Chinese plants, more resistant to cold, are found in the higher plantations of northern Darjeeling where some bushes grow on sloping terrain over 6,000 feet high. In the southern plantations, which lie at lower elevations, the Assam plant likes the plentiful rainfall. Darjeeling's 102 gardens produce approximately 16,534.7 tons per year. The pickers, always women, start gathering the leaves in the early morning and sometimes work on terraced slopes that climb steadily upwards at an angle of 45 degrees.

Because of the climate and high elevations, Darjeeling tea bushes do not go

Clonal tea plantation in Darjeeling.

on growing throughout the year. The teas are picked from April to October, when the period of winter dormancy begins and growing stops. New growth begins in March after the first light showers of spring. This is the first flush. The second flush is gathered in May and June. The monsoon, which reaches the area in the middle of June and continues until the end of September, brings a total of 9 feet 9 inches–16 feet 3 inches of rainfall. The teas produced during this period contain a lot of moisture and are of standard quality. The leaves are processed by the orthodox method of manufacture and have a brownish, black, well-twisted appearance with plenty of golden tip.

FIRST FLUSH DARJEELING

The Darjeeling bushes' first new shoots—the first flush—are plucked in April. These first teas of the season are much sought after, and fetch incredibly high prices in the world auctions, with wealthy Indian buyers competing with international brokers for this very special tea. Some of the best first flush Darjeelings go to Germany, where they have been highly prized since the 1960s, and to Russia. First flush Darjeelings are often marketed and imported rather like Beaujolais Nouveau wines. The new supply of the eagerly awaited harvest is air-freighted to consuming countries two to four weeks after manufacture (four weeks or more before it would normally become available) and served at special tea tastings and afternoon teas that attract widespread publicity.

Castleton First Flush

Characteristics

Perfect green-brown leaf with plenty of tips from one of the most prestigious gardens in the area. Gives an exquisite perfume and taste of green muscatel.

Brewing hints

Brew 1½ teaspoons in a scant 1 cup water at 203°F. Infuse for 2–3 minutes.

Drinking recommendations

Drink without milk as an afternoon tea. Pairs perfectly with smoked salmon, and with fresh strawberries and cream.

Tea pickers in Darjeeling.

Bloomfield First Flush

Characteristics

An exquisite tea from this recognized garden. Beautiful leaf showing plenty of white tip. Its subtle astringent flavor is typical of Darjeeling first flush.

Brewing hints

Brew 1½ teaspoons in a scant 1 cup water at 203°F. Infuse for 2–3 minutes.

Drinking recommendations

An afternoon tea. Drink without milk.

Other recommended gardens

Ambootia, Badamtam, Balasun, Gielle, Goomtee, Gopaldhara, Kalej Valley, Lingia, Millikthong, Mim, Namring, Orange Valley, Pandam, Seeyok, Singtom, Soureni, Springside, and Thurbo.

Margaret's Hope

Characteristics

A highly prized tea from a famous garden. Very attractive tippy, green-brown leaf that gives a very clear bright infusion and a gentle delicate flavor.

Brewing hints

Brew 1 teaspoon in a scant 1 cup water at 203°F. Infuse for 2–3 minutes.

Drinking recommendations

An afternoon tea. Drink without milk.

"IN-BETWEEN" DARJEELINGS

Darjeeling's "In-Between" teas are gathered in April and May, and produce a flavor that marries the greenness and astringency of the young first flush leaves with the more rounded maturity of the second flush teas that are picked in early summer. These teas are not widely available but worth trying if they can be found. Drink without milk.

SECOND FLUSH DARJEELING

Second flush Darjeelings are picked during May and June, and produce excellent quality teas that are considered by many to be better than the first flush and the best that Darjeeling produces. These teas have a rounder, fruitier, more mature, less astringent flavor than the earlier teas. The leaves are darker brown and contain plenty of silvery tip.

Namring

Characteristics
Beautiful leaves that give a fruity, balanced taste.

Brewing hints
Brew 1 teaspoon in a scant 1 cup water at 203°F. Infuse for 3 minutes.

Drinking recommendations

An afternoon tea for special occasions. Drink without or with a little milk.

Puttabong

Characteristics
Very smooth liquor with marked muscatel flavor. This is one of the best second flush Darjeelings available.

Brewing hints
Brew 1 teaspoon in a scant 1 cup water at 203°F. Infuse for 3 minutes.

Drinking recommendations

An all-day tea, drink without milk.

Other recommended gardens
Badamtam, Balasun, Bannockburn, Castleton, Gielle, Glenburn, Jungpana, Kalej Valley, Lingia, Makaibari organic, Moondakotee, Nagri, Phoobsering, Risheehat, Singbulli, Snowview, Soom, Teesta Valley, Tongsong, and Tukdah.

DARJEELING AUTUMNALS

Autumnals are gathered in October and November, and give very good quality dark brown leaves after processing. The infusion is copper-colored, much darker than the earlier teas.

Margaret's Hope

Characteristics
Large dark brown leaf that gives a rounded flavor, with plenty of body, and a wonderful aroma.

Brewing hints
Brew 1 teaspoon in a scant 1 cup water at 203°F. Infuse for 3 minutes.

Drinking recommendations
Drink without or with a little milk throughout the day.

Other recommended gardens
Sungma and Pussimbing.

DARJEELING BLEND

Teas from different plucking seasons and from a variety of Darjeeling gardens are blended to give the unique flavor, wonderful aroma, and high quality that the area is famous for.

Darjeeling Blend

Characteristics
A delicate mixture of teas from the best gardens that gives a light infusion with a delicate characteristic muscatel flavor and pronounced aroma.

Brewing hints
Brew 1 teaspoon in a scant 1 cup water at 203°F. Infuse for 3 minutes.

Drinking recommendations
An afternoon tea. Drink without or with a little milk.

A box of fine quality Darjeeling tea.

DARJEELING GREEN

Although Darjeeling produces mainly black tea, because of the interest in the health benefits of green tea drinking, there are expectations of a growth in demand of quality green teas. Darjeeling is just one of India's tea growing areas that are now producing green tea.

DOOARS

Dooars is a tiny province to the west of Assam. The low-grown teas it produces are dark and full bodied but with less character than Assams. They are good day-time teas that drink well in the morning or with afternoon tea.

Ayra

Characteristics
A rare tea from a well-known garden. Gives an infusion a little like Japanese Sencha. An exquisite aroma, delicate taste, and gentle on the palate.

Brewing hints
Brew 2 teaspoons in a scant 1 cup water at 158°F. Infuse for 3 minutes.

Drinking recommendations
Drink without milk as a digestif or a refreshing drink at any time of the day.

Good Hope

Characteristics
Fresh, flowery, good-colored infusion.

Brewing hints
Brew 1 teaspoon in a scant 1 cup water at 203°F. Infuse for 3–4 minutes.

Drinking recommendations
A day-time tea that supports a little milk.

Other recommended gardens
Risheehat.

NILGIRI

The Nilgiris, or Blue Mountains, are a stunningly beautiful range of hills that stretch down the southwestern tip of India from the state of Kerala, another tea-growing area, to the state of Tamil Nadu. Among the peaks and foothills, there are rolling grasslands and dense jungles where elephants roam in herds. The tea industry was established in this area in 1840 when Colonel John Ouchterloney R.E., while surveying below the Nilgiris, came upon a sheet of virgin forest well-supplied with its own rivers and streams. At a height of about 4,500 feet and with approximately 80 inches of rain a year, it was the perfect situation for tea and coffee growing. Ouchterloney's brother, James, planted it, imported labor and food, and started production. Ootacamund, the famous hill resort, lies in these hills and is affectionately

The Nilgiri Queen chugging through Glendale Estate, Nilgiri.

Typical Nilgiri tea field with shady trees and jungle border.

known as "Ooty" by local planters and tourists who visit throughout the year.

Today, there are about 61,776 acres of tea bushes growing at elevations varying from 1,000 to 6,000 feet among eucalyptus, cypresses, and blue gum trees. They produce about 61,729.5 tons of tea annually, making the area India's second biggest tea-producing region after Assam. Every plateau, slope, and valley is covered with bushes which crop all year round. Most of the plantations get two monsoons a year, so the

bushes have two major flushing periods, in April/May when about 25 percent of the annual crop is gathered, and September/December when a further 35–40 percent is plucked. Further picking goes on throughout the year. It is these conditions that give the tea its unique flavor.

Nilgiri produces fine flavory teas with bright, brisk liquors, and a smooth rounded mellow flavor. Because of their strength, they are ideal for blending with lighter teas that give flavor but not body.

Nunsuch

Characteristics
Large-leafed tea which gives a fruity, bright, flavorful brew.

Brewing hints
Brew 1 teaspoon in a scant 1 cup water at 203°F. Infuse for 3–4 minutes.

Drinking recommendations

Drink all day with a little milk.

Other recommended gardens
Chamraj, Corsley, Havukal, Pascoes Woodlands, Tigerhill, and Tungmullay.

SIKKIM
This small Indian state produces teas of similar character to Darjeeling teas but with more body and a fruity flavor. Very few are exported however, so they may be hard to find.

Temi

Characteristics
Very high quality orthodox Darjeeling-type tea, with beautiful leaves, and plenty of golden tips. Scented liquor with a fruity, almost honeyed flavor.

Brewing hints
Brew 1 teaspoon in a scant 1 cup water at 203°F. Infuse for 3 minutes.

Drinking recommendations

A special occasion tea. Drink alone or with a little milk.

TERAI

Terai tea is grown on the plain that lies just south of Darjeeling. The tea gives a rich-colored brew with a pronounced spicy taste, which is often used in blends.

Ord

Characteristics
Good pale, coppery infusion and strong flavor.

Brewing hints
Brew 1 teaspoon in a scant 1 cup water at 203°F. Infuse for 3–4 minutes.

Drinking recommendations
Drink with milk as a morning tea.

TRAVANCORE

Travancore lies at a similar altitude to Sri Lanka and produces teas with similar characteristics, while also providing a reminder of the teas of northern India.

Highgrown

Characteristics
Coppery liquor with strong, full, slightly earthy flavor.

Brewing hints
Brew 1 teaspoon in a scant 1 cup water at 203°F. Infuse for 3–4 minutes.

Drinking recommendations
Drink with a little milk as a breakfast tea.

SOUTHERN INDIAN TEAS

Teas from other southern areas of India—Kerala, Madras, and Mysore—tend to be marketed as Travancores. The Tea Board of India only promotes Darjeelings, Assams, and Nilgiris as specialty, self-drinking teas.

All the tea-producing areas of South India are located in hilly terrain and consist of about 40,000 smallholdings. Production reaches 192,904.6 tons of made tea per year 25 percent of which goes to export markets.

SRI LANKA

*Teas from the highest region on the island are described as the 'champagne'
of Ceylon teas.*

UNTIL THE 1860s, THE MAIN CROP PRODUCED on the island of Sri Lanka, then Ceylon, was coffee. But in 1869, the coffee-rust fungus, *Hemileia vastatrix*, killed the majority of the coffee plants and estate owners had to diversify into other crops in order to avoid total ruin. The owners of Loolecondera Estate had been interested in tea since the late 1850s and, in 1866, James Taylor, a recently arrived Scot, was selected to be in charge of the first sowing of tea seeds in 1867, on 19 acres of land.

INDIA

ARABIAN SEA

Kandy

Dimbula

COLOMBO

UVA

Nuwara Eliya

Adam's Peak

BAY OF BENGAL

Ratnapura

Galle

Taylor had acquired some basic knowledge of tea cultivation in North India and made some initial experiments in manufacture, using his bungalow verandah as the factory and rolling the leaf by hand on tables. Firing of the oxidized leaf was carried out on clay stoves over charcoal fires with the leaf on wire trays. His first teas were sold locally and were declared delicious. By 1872, Taylor had a fully equipped factory, and, in 1873, his first quality teas were sold for a very good price at the London auction. Through his dedication and determination, Taylor was largely responsible for the early success of the tea crop in Ceylon. Between 1873 and 1880, production rose from just 23 pounds to 81.3 tons, and by 1890, to 22,899.8 tons.

Most of the Ceylon tea gardens are situated at elevations between 3,000 and 8,000 feet in two areas of the southwestern part of the island, to the east of Colombo and in the Galle district on the southern point. In the hot, steamy plains and foothills, the tea bushes flush every seven or eight days and are picked all year round. The finest teas are gathered from late June to the end of August in eastern districts and from the beginning of February to mid-March in the western parts.

Until 1971, more than 80 percent of the island's tea estates were owned and managed by British companies. In 1971, the Sri Lankan government introduced a Land

Tea pickers gathering leaves into their baskets.

Reform Act which gave the state control of the majority of the plantations (which also grow rubber and coconuts for export)—leaving about one-third in private hands. Since 1990, a restructuring program has been going on to involve the private sector companies (both Sri Lankan and foreign) as Managing Agents of the state-owned plantations. The long-term aim is for the private managing companies to take on most, if not all, of the financial responsibility and control of the estates, with the government retaining ownership.

Extreme political, industrial, and economic problems over the past years have meant that Sri Lanka has fallen from the position of number one producer in the world to number eight in 1993. Producers are having to face major decisions regarding production methods, product range, and export markets. Although the U.K. was once Sri Lanka's biggest customer, almost 70 percent of production now goes to Russia, the Middle East, and North Africa. The Arab market used to prefer orthodox teas but consumers there are steadily moving towards European tastes and are demanding more tea in tea bags. Sri Lanka's fine orthodox teas, considered by many to be among the best teas in the world, are not suitable for tea bags. Only 3 percent of production in 1993 was CTC and producers are having to decide whether to convert to CTC production in order to reach a wider market. Some manufacturers think that there will always be a market for the orthodox teas; others think that CTC is the best way forward. New customers are also being sought for the increasing range of packeted teas—in sachets, cartons, economy packs, reed ware, basket packs, soft wood boxes, tins, and canisters—that are now available. Products containing 100 percent Ceylon tea are now using the Lion logo, developed by the Ceylon Tea Board, that guarantees the country of origin and protects the image of Sri Lanka's quality teas.

Ceylon Tea's lion logo.

Sri Lanka's finest teas are produced mainly from bushes that grow above 4,000 feet. The bushes grow more slowly in the cooler, mistier climate, and are harder to harvest because of the steep angle of the slopes on which they are planted.

There are six main tea-producing areas. Galle, to the south of the island; Ratnapura, about 55 miles east of the capital Colombo; Kandy, the low region near the ancient royal capital; Nuwara Eliya, the highest area that produces the finest teas; Dimbula, west of the central mountains; and Uva, located east of Dimbula.

The teas produced in each region have their own individual characteristics of flavor, aroma, and color. Low-grown teas, produced at 1,500 to 1,800 feet, are of good quality and give good color and strength but lack the distinctive flavor and bright fresh taste of the higher-grown teas and are usually used in blending. Mid-grown teas, grown between 1,800 and 3,500 feet, are rich in flavor and give good color. High-grown teas, from heights of between 3,500 and 7,500 feet, are the very best that Sri Lanka produces, giving a beautiful golden liquor and an intense powerful flavor. As well as the wonderful black teas, some estates also produce silver tip white tea that gives a very pale straw-colored liquor and should be drunk without milk. All Sri Lanka's black teas are best drunk with a little milk.

DIMBULA

Like Nuwara Eliya, Dimbula is drenched by the monsoon during August and September and produces its best teas during the dry months of January and February. The teas are noted for their body and strength, and a powerful aroma.

Kenilworth

Characteristics
Long, wiry beautiful leaves that give an exquisite taste, almost oaky, with body and strength.

Brewing hints
Brew 1 teaspoon in a scant 1 cup water at 203°F. Infuse for 3–4 minutes.

Drinking recommendations
Drink with milk as an afternoon tea.

Other recommended gardens
Diyagama, Loinorn, Pettiagalla, Redalla, Somerset, Strathspey, and Theresia.

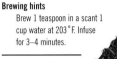

GALLE

This area, in the south of the island, specializes in Flowery Orange Pekoes and Orange Pekoes that have well-produced, regular-size leaf and give an amber golden liquor with a scented aroma and a fine, gentle, subtle taste.

Allen Valley

Characteristics
Beautiful leaf that gives a smooth, perfumed liquor.

Brewing hints
Brew 1 teaspoon in a scant 1 cup water at 203°F. Infuse for 3–4 minutes.

Drinking recommendations

Drink with milk as an afternoon tea.

Devonia

Characteristics
A very well-made leaf giving a beautiful golden infusion with subtle perfumed taste.

Brewing hints
Brew 1 teaspoon in a scant 1 cup water at 203°F. Infuse for 3–4 minutes.

Drinking recommendations

Excellent with afternoon tea, taken with a little milk.

Galaboda

Characteristics
Regular-shaped leaf that gives a beautiful liquor with good color, wonderful aroma, and a rich mellow taste.

Brewing hints
Brew 1 teaspoon in a scant 1 cup water at 203°F. Infuse for 3–4 minutes.

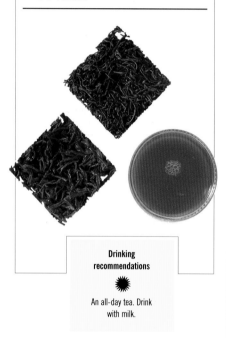

Drinking recommendations

An all-day tea. Drink with milk.

Other recommended gardens
Berubeula.

NUWARA ELIYA

Teas from the highest region on the island are often described as the "champagne" of Ceylon teas. The leaf is gathered all year round, but the finest teas are made from that plucked in January and February. The best teas of the area give a rich, golden, excellent quality liquor that is smooth, bright, and delicately perfumed.

Ceylon tea picker.

Nuwara Eliya Estate

Characteristics
Bright brisk flavor and wonderful perfume.

Brewing hints
Brew 1 teaspoon in a scant 1 cup water at 203°F. Infuse for 3–4 minutes.

Drinking recommendations

✴

Good at any time of the day with a little milk.

Other recommended gardens
Gastotte, Lovers Leap, and Tommagong.

RATNAPURA

Ratnapura produces low-grown teas that are mainly used in blends, but also drink well alone with a little milk.

Ratnapura

Characteristics
Long-leafed tea that gives a slightly sweet aroma and a gentle smooth taste.

Brewing hints
Brew 1 teaspoon in a scant 1 cup water at 203°F. Infuse for 3–4 minutes.

Drinking recommendations

🫖

Drink with milk as an afternoon tea.

UVA

Uva, on the eastern slopes of the central mountains, produces teas with a distinctive mellow flavor whose reputation stretches world-wide. The best teas are plucked between June and September. The dry wind that blows towards Uva during this period gives the teas their fine taste and aroma.

Saint James

Characteristics
Copper-colored infusion with a very smooth, pronounced taste and wonderful aroma.

Brewing hints
Brew 1 teaspoon in a scant 1 cup water at 203°F. Infuse for 3–4 minutes.

Drinking recommendations
A breakfast or day-time tea. Drink with milk.

Other recommended gardens
Adawatte, Aislaby, Attempettia, Blairmond, Bombagalla, Dyraaba, High Forest, and Uva Highlands

CEYLON BLENDS

Following a tradition that was established at the end of the nineteenth century by Sir Thomas Lipton, several companies still market blended Ceylon teas as Ceylon Orange Pekoe or Ceylon BOP, sometimes also by estate name, sometimes not. A good blend will give a bright, rich, coppery liquor with a brisk fresh flavor. In order to be sure of buying 100 percent Ceylon blended teas when buying pre-packed teas, look for the Ceylon Tea Board Lion logo.

A flourishing tea bush.

THE
FAR
EAST

CHINA

*The widest range in the world of the finest quality teas,
many still made by hand.*

C OMMERCIAL CULTIVATION OF TEA in China began well before the birth of Christ and in the past, Chinese merchants recognized more than 8,000 different types of tea—classified by the five different methods of manufacture, two grades of quality of manufacture, four different leaf grades, and 200 place names. Tea crops were grown wherever a peasant or farmer had space on the family smallholding.

Pan-firing teas by hand in seventeenth century China.

Until the late nineteenth century, techniques used for tea cultivation were much the same as they had always been. Seeds were collected in October, germinated through the winter months, then planted out during the spring rains in neat rows. Larger plantations were laid out on north- and east-facing hillsides, and millet and corn were grown amongst the tea bushes to provide shade. During the colder winter months, straw was tied around the bushes to protect them from frost. An ancient Chinese proverb says that "The finest teas come from high mountains" and this is true, but it did not stop the Chinese from growing tea everywhere, even on the outskirts of busy towns as well as in extremely inaccessible and isolated locations.

A description by Robert Fortune in his book *A Journey to the Tea Countries of China*, published in 1852, gives a good idea of how the tea was processed:

"In the harvest seasons, are seen little family groups on the side of every hill, when the weather is dry, engaged in gathering the tea leaves . . . The drying pans and furnaces are of iron, round and shallow, and, in fact, are the same or nearly the same, which the natives have in general use for cooking their rice.

The pans become hot very soon after the warm air has begun to circulate in the flue beneath them. A quantity of leaves, from a sieve or basket, are now thrown into the pans, and turned over and shaken up. The leaves are immediately affected by the heat. This part of the process lasts about five minutes in which time the leaves lose their crispness and become soft and pliable. They are then taken out of the pans and thrown upon a table, the upper part of which is made of split bamboo . . . three or four persons now surround the table, and the heap of leaves is divided into many parcels, each individual taking as many as he can hold in his hands, and the rolling process commences . . ."

Since the cultural revolution, tea co-operatives have been established and the tea industry rationalized, with mechanization being introduced in most factories to replace the age-old hand methods. In some places, however, skilled hand production still goes on.

Today, tea is grown in 18 regions, Anhui, Fujian, Gansu, Guangdong, Guizhou, Hainan, Henan, Hubei, Hunan, Jiangsu, Jiangxi, Shaanxi, Shandong, Sichuan, Yunnan, Zhejiang, Tibet, and Guangxi Zhuang. The most important regions are Zhejiang, Hunan, Sichuan, Fujian, and Anhui. Production is a state-controlled monopoly and packages give precise details as to which office of which branch of which company was responsible for the manufacture and marketing of the particular tea in the package.

These state co-operatives produce good quality black, oolong, and green teas that are generally blended to give standard quality every year. Some of these standard teas are of excellent quality and are mostly exported.

Separating the leaves before firing.

About 80 percent of annual production is of green teas for the domestic market. Most black and oolong teas are designed for the export market, and are sold through direct contact with tea companies rather than through the auctions.

China's "first crop" teas are plucked from mid-April to mid-May. This harvest is thought to give the finest quality tea, and produce roughly 55 percent of annual production. The second crop is picked in

Tea garden in Sichuan.

early summer and a third autumn crop is harvested in some areas.

China teas are not normally sold by garden name but rather by names that denote the method of manufacture and quality. Names can be confusing since a mixture of Fukienese (from Fujian Province), Cantonese, and standard Chinese has been used for tea over the centuries. Each province tends to have its own name for each tea, its own spelling, and its own pronunciation. Consequently, names that look and sound completely different often refer to exactly the same tea. An additional problem is caused by the fact that even in Chinese, one tea may have more than one name—its main name, its historical or legendary name, and a name that gives additional geographical information.

So, a tea that is marketed in the West as Chunmee (and also as Chun Mei) is Zhenmei in Pinyin, Janmei in Cantonese, and is often known as Eyebrow Tea because of the appearance of the processed leaf. And Pingshui Gunpowder, manufactured at Pingshui, a town in Shanghai, in Chinese Pinyin is Pinshui Zhucha (which means Pearl Tea, referring to the pellet-shaped balls of tea), and in Cantonese Ping Shui Chue Cha.

As well as the individual names, each tea made available on the market also bears a grade number that indicates that the tea conforms to a given standard. This means that the tea can be purchased without prior sampling, and buyers can also rest assured that if a tea does not come up to the given standard, it is not marketed.

Export of China's teas is gaining momentum with increased interest among tea connoisseurs who have recently discovered the amazing variety of types and flavors and recognize their very fine qualities. Exports rose from 151,016 tons in 1989 to more than 225,973.6 tons in the early 1990s. Tea is China's third most important export after silk and grain. It's largest markets are Morocco, the U.S., Tunisia, Poland, Hong Kong, Russia, C.I.S. countries, and the U.K. Sales in the U.S. are increasing steadily and rare China teas are now finding a place in mail-order catalogs and in tea retail outlets which offer not just the blacks and oolongs but also the rarer white teas such as Silver Dragon, and green teas with exotic names such as Tiantai Cloud and Mist, Supreme Dragon Well, several types of Jasmine tea, and compressed teas such as Tuo tea and Pu-erh. Pu-erh tea is generally sold for its medicinal qualities. It is thought to be good for treating diarrhea, indigestion, and high cholesterol levels. It is an oolong, semi-fermented tea which is sold in several different forms, including bowl-shaped cakes and tea balls (see pages 160–1).

Sorting tea in a factory in Anxi.

CHINA WHITE TEAS

Pai Mu Tan Imperial (Balmudan, White Peony)

This rare white tea is made from very small buds and leaves that are plucked in the early spring, just before they open. When they have been steamed and dried, they have the appearance of lots of miniature bunches of small white blossoms with tiny leaves.

Characteristics

This white tea comes from Fujian Province and gives a clear, pale infusion with a fresh aroma and a smooth velvety flavor.

Brewing hints

Brew 2 teaspoons in a scant 1 cup water at 185°F. Infuse for 7 minutes.

Drinking recommendations

Drink without milk or sugar, after meals as a healthy digestif, or as a light afternoon tea.

Yin Zhen (Yinfeng, Silver Needles)

This tea, also from Fujian Province, is made from tender new buds that are covered in silver-white hairs. Because of its silvery appearance, white tea is sometimes sold as Silvery Tip Pekoe, China White, or Fujian White.

Characteristics

This is the perfect white tea. The leaves, that really do look like silver needles, are picked on only two days a year and are processed entirely by hand. It is very expensive but wonderful.

Brewing hints

Brew 2 teaspoons in a scant 1 cup water at 185°F. Infuse for 15 minutes.

Drinking recommendations

An all-day tea. Drink alone, without milk or sugar as a refreshing digestif.

CHINA GREEN TEAS

Chun Mee (Chun Mei, Zhenmei, Precious Eyebrows)

It is the shape of the processed leaves that gives this tea its name. The processing of "eyebrow" teas demands great skill in order to hand roll the leaves to the correct shape at the right temperature for the correct length of time.

Characteristics

Long, fine jade leaves that give a clear, pale yellow liquor with a smooth taste. Popular among China's foreign customers for many years.

Brewing hints

Brew 2 teaspoons in a scant 1 cup water at 158°F. Infuse for 3–4 minutes.

Drinking recommendations

Drink alone or with mint as a refreshing all-day drink

Gunpowder (Zhucha, Pearl Tea)

The name is said to come from the fact that the tightly rolled balls of tea resemble pellets of gunpowder. Most Gunpowder tea is produced in Pingshui in Zhejian Province and surrounding counties.

Characteristics

Tiny pellets open up in hot water to give a strong, greeny-coppery liquor with a pungent taste.

Brewing hints

Brew generous 1–2 teaspoons pellets in a pot of water at 158–176°F. Infuse for 3–4 minutes.

Drinking recommendations

Drink alone in the afternoon or evening or use for iced tea, flavored with lemon and sugar, or with mint and sugar (as in Morocco)

Lung Ching (Longjing, Dragon's Well)

This famous tea is produced in Zhejiang Province, in a village called Dragon Well, to the west of West Lake. The tea won a gold medal with Palms at the 1988 meeting of the International Institute for Quality Selection.

Characteristics

Tea mentioned by Lu Yu and famous for its flat, green leaves, its jade green color, and its delicious aroma and mellow flavor. The liquor is clear yellow with a slightly sweet aftertaste.

Brewing hints

Brew 2 teaspoons in a scant 1 cup water at 158°F. Infuse for 3 minutes.

Drinking recommendations

Drink alone as a refreshing all-day tea, or as a digestif after a heavy meal.

Pi Lo Chun (Biluochun, Green Snail Spring)

This is a rare tea that is known all over the world for its snail-like appearance. The bushes grow among peach, plum, and apricot trees so the young leaves absorb the fragrance of the fruit blossoms. Pluckers take only one leaf with each new bud.

Characteristics

Leaves and buds are rolled by hand to form tiny snail-like spirals, covered in fine silver hairs. The yellow-green liquor has a unique clean, fresh, slightly sweet flavor.

Brewing hints

Brew 2 teaspoons in a scant 1 cup water at 158°F. Infuse for 3–4 minutes.

Drinking recommendations

Drink alone on very special occasions, not just because of its high price but also for its distinguished quality.

Xinyang Maojian

The misty, cloudy climate of the mountainous Xinyang area of Henan Province produces tea with a fine fresh aroma and a subtle aftertaste. The leaves are skillfully rolled by hand.

Characteristics
Fine, taut strips of leaf that give an orangy-green infusion with a fresh aroma and a smooth taste.

Brewing hints
Brew 2 teaspoons in a scant 1 cup water at 158°F. Infuse for 3 minutes.

Drinking recommendations
✪

A special occasion green tea. Drink without milk or sugar.

Taiping Houkui (Tai Ping Hau Fui)

This is the best of Anhui Province's green teas. Although not officially a scented tea, the leaves absorb the flavor of the millions of orchids that grow wild on the mountain as the tea bushes are beginning to open their new leaves. The tea won a gold medal in 1915 at the Panama Pacific International Exhibition and is world famous.

Characteristics
The dark green, straight, pointed leaves open out in hot water to reveal pink veins. They give a delicious orchid-flavored taste.

Brewing hints
Brew 2 teaspoons in a scant 1 cup water at 158°F. Infuse for 3 minutes.

Drinking recommendations
🍵

A light subtle afternoon tea. Drink without milk or sugar.

Other recommended China green teas Dong Yang Dong Bai, Gaungdong, Guo Gu Nao, Huang Shan Mao Feng, Hu Bei, Hunan Green, Hyson, Pai Hou, Son Yang Ying Hao, and White Downy.

CHINA OOLONG TEAS

Fonghwang Tan-chung (Fenghuang Dancong, Fenghuang Select)

The leaves for this tea come from tall straight-trunked trees and are gathered with the use of long ladders. The local Chinese brew the tea strong in tiny pots. For the first infusion they steep the leaves for just one minute, for the second, three minutes, and for the third, five minutes.

Characteristics
Long golden strips of leaf that turn green in water, with reddish-brown edges. The liquor is pale orangy-brown and the first infusion can be bitter. A second infusion is more mellow.

Brewing hints
Brew 1 teaspoon in a scant 1 cup water at 203°F. Infuse for 5–7 minutes.

Drinking recommendations

(

An excellent, refined tea. Drink in the evening.

Shui Hsien (Shuixian, Water Sprite)

The strain of the tea tree whose leaves are used to manufacture Shui Hsien is a tall, large-leafed, single-trunked tree. The leaves are dark, shiny green and the buds fat, yellowy-green, and covered in hairs. They are used to make both black and white teas in Fujian Province.

Characteristics
Loose twisted strips of leaf give a clear orangy-brown liquor with a gentle slightly spicy flavor.

Brewing hints
Brew 1 teaspoon in a scant 1 cup water at 203°F. Infuse for 5–7 minutes.

Drinking recommendations

Drink without milk or sugar in the morning or throughout the day.

Ti Kwan Yin (Tieguanyin, Tea of the Iron Goddess of Mercy)

This very special tea also comes from Fujian Province. One explanation of the name is that the iron goddess of mercy is said to have appeared in a dream to a local farmer and told him to look in the cave behind her temple. There he found a single tea shoot which he planted and cultivated. This is one of China's most sought-after teas.

Characteristics
Stout, crinkly leaves that unfurl in boiling water to give greeny-brown lace-edged leaves. The infusion is brownish-green with an aromatic gentle flavor.

Brewing hints
Place 1 teaspoon in a pot and pour in water at 203°F. Immediately pour off the water and let the leaves breathe for a moment or two. Then refill the pot with boiling water and steep the leaves for 3–5 minutes. The leaves will give several infusions.

Drinking recommendations
✡

A very special tea for very special occasions. Drink alone without milk or sugar.

Pouchong (Pao Zhong, Baozhong)

The name for this very lightly fermented tea comes from the fact that the leaves were originally wrapped in paper during fermentation. It originates from Fujian Province and the method of manufacture was transposed to Taiwan.

Characteristics
Long, stylish black leaf that brews a very mild cup with an amber infusion, smooth flavor, and a very smooth, sweet taste.

Brewing hints
Brew 1 teaspoon in a scant 1 cup water at 203°F. Infuse for 5–7 minutes.

Drinking recommendations
🫖 ☾

Drink without milk as an afternoon or evening tea.

Other recommended China oolongs
China Fujian Dark Oolong, Dahongpao, Oolong Sechung, and Wuyi Liu Hsiang (Liuxiang).

CHINA BLACK TEAS

Tea taster at work in a Keemun tasting room.

Keemun

In 1915 Keemun won a gold medal at the Panama Pacific International Exhibition. Grown in Anhui Province it is a "gonfu" or "congou" tea—which means that it is made with disciplined skill (*gongfu*) to produce the thin tight strips of leaf without breaking the leaves.

Characteristics
The tight black leaves give a rich brown liquor, which has a lightly scented flavor and a delicate aroma.

Brewing hints
Brew 1 teaspoon in a scant 1 cup water at 203°F. Infuse for 5–7 minutes.

Drinking recommendations

Excellent with lightly spiced foods and as a digestif. Drink without milk or sugar. A perfect evening tea.

Keemun tea bushes.

Keemun Mao Feng

Mao Feng means "hairpoint," denoting even finer strips of hand-rolled leaf than those found in standard Keemun.

Characteristics
The rarest of Keemun teas with beautiful well-made leaves that give a delicate, very fine flavor.

Brewing hints
Brew 1 teaspoon in a scant 1 cup water at 203 °F. Infuse for 5–7 minutes.

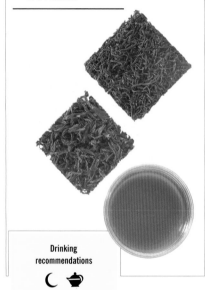

Drinking recommendations

(C ☕

An evening or afternoon tea to accompany very light foods.

Lapsang Souchong (Zengshan Xiaozhong)

Smoked teas are a specialty of Fujian Province. The leaves are withered over pine fires then pan-fried and rolled. They are then pressed into barrels and covered with cloths. After fermenting, they are fired and then rolled, and placed in bamboo baskets and dried over smoking pine fires.

Characteristics
Thick black strips of leaf give a distinct smoky aroma and flavor, and a rich red liquor.

Brewing hints
Brew 1 teaspoon in a scant 1 cup water at 203 °F. Infuse for 5–7 minutes.

Drinking recommendations

) ❚❚

Drink without or with a little milk. Pairs very well with English breakfast foods and with fish.

Other recommended smoked China teas
Tarry Souchong and Yo Pao.

Jiuqu Wulong (Black Dragon)

The name Jiuqu means Nine-bend Stream, the area that this tea comes from. This is a fully-fermented "gonfu" black tea, but because of its name it is sometimes wrongly labeled an oolong.

Characteristics
Fine, tight twists of leaf that give a coppery red liquor with a mellow, subtle refreshing taste.

Brewing hints
Brew 1 teaspoon in a scant 1 cup water at 203°F. Infuse for 5–7 minutes.

Drinking recommendations

Drink without milk as an afternoon or evening tea.

Szechwan Imperial

Some black teas from China, like this one, are marketed simply by the name of the province in which they are produced. Others include Guangdong Black, Hainan Black, Hunan Black, and Fujian Black.

Characteristics
Fine tippy leaves that give a deep-colored liquor, a gentle aroma, and a smooth almost sweet, scented flavor.

Brewing hints
Brew 1 teaspoon in a scant 1 cup water at 203°F. Infuse for 5–7 minutes.

Drinking recommendations

An afternoon tea, taken without milk.

Yunnan (Dianhong)

Yunnan has been a tea-producing province for more than 1,700 years and the tea plant is thought to be a native of the area. The trees used to make Yunnan black teas produce fat buds and shoots and thick soft leaves.

Characteristics
Black leaves with plenty of golden buds that give a slightly peppery brisk liquor and a pronounced aroma.

Brewing hints
Brew 1 teaspoon in a scant 1 cup water at 203°F. Infuse for 5–7 minutes.

Drinking recommendations
)🍴 🍵

Will take a little milk and drinks well as a breakfast or afternoon tea.

Other recommended China black teas
Ching Wo, Ning Chow, and Panyong.

CHINA COMPRESSED TEAS

Tuancha (Tea Balls)

These balls of tea are made in different sizes, the smallest being about the size of a table tennis ball.

Characteristics
Little balls of tea with an earthy flavor and aroma.

Brewing hints
Use 5 cups water for each ball. Infuse in boiling water for 5–7 minutes.

Drinking recommendations
🍃 ☀

Drink without milk at any time as a light refreshing drink, especially after a meal.

Tuancha.

Tuocha

Originally from Yunnan Province, compressed tea shaped like a bird's nest is molded by pressing the leaves into a bowl.

Characteristics
Looks like a small bird's nest and gives the same, earthy, elemental taste as other Pu-erh teas.

Brewing hints
Break off a scant 1 teaspoon per cup and infuse in boiling water for 5 minutes. Strain into cups.

Dschuan Cha (Brick Tea)

This is more a decorative item than for use in brewing. It is made by hydraulically compressing black tea dust.

Characteristics
Not a tea with any special qualities. More curiosity value than fine flavor.

Brewing hints
Infuse a scant 1 teaspoon per cup in boiling water for 3–4 minutes. Strain into cups.

Drinking recommendations

An all-day tea. Drink with or without milk.

Drinking recommendations

Drink without milk as a digestif after meals or at any time of day or evening.

Tea brick.

INDONESIA

Teas which are light and offer good flavor.

S ET IN THE SOUTH CHINA SEA and the Pacific Ocean, Indonesia is a chain of islands that stretch from Malaysia to Papua New Guinea. Java and Sumatra, the two biggest islands, are where the main tea plantations are located. In the early seventeenth century, the Dutch conducted their trade in Chinese commodities, including tea, from Java, and the Dutch East India Company was responsible for establishing the first tea plantations on the island in the early eighteenth century. Initially they used seeds from China, but these did not flourish, so they have latterly used Assam bushes from India.

Tea pickers in Java, Indonesia.

The crop was later introduced to Sumatra and, in recent years, production has started on Sulawesi Island. Until the Second World War, Indonesia black teas, along with those of India and Ceylon, dominated the European and British markets. However the war left the island's industry devastated, and tea production was minimal until 1984 when a rehabilitation program started. The establishment of the Tea Board of Indonesia has helped in the restructuring of the industry, the refurbishment of factories, the rehabilitation of plantations with superior cloned tea plants, an improvement in facilities and increased production.

In the past, only black orthodox teas were produced, but the demand for quick-brewing tea bag teas has prompted producers to switch to CTC production. There are now 16 factories producing more than 16,534.7 tons of tea per year, most of which is exported. Green tea production was introduced in 1988, and is expected to increase in the coming years because of the growing recognition of the health benefits of green-tea consumption and a wider international interest. At present, most of the green tea is mixed with jasmine flowers and reprocessed as jasmine tea, mainly for the domestic market. It is consumed mostly as a soft drink that is marketed in cartons and bottles.

On Java, estates account for about 33,838 acres under tea, with Sumatra and the other islands accounting for another 147,423 acres. The bushes flush all year, due to dry, clement conditions, but the best teas are gathered in July, August, and September. Production is now approximately 60 percent green and 40 percent black. Most of the black teas are sold for export through the weekly Jakarta auctions. Traditional markets have always been the U.K., the U.S., The Netherlands, Australia, the Middle East, Germany, Pakistan, Singapore, and Japan, while Russia, C.I.S. countries, and Poland have recently started purchasing. Over the last eight to ten years, exports have climbed steadily, increasing from only 93,696.4 tons in 1984. In 1992, Indonesia exported 132,277.2 tons of tea, an estimated 12 percent of total world exports.

Indonesian teas are light and offer good flavor. Most are sold for blending tea bags or loose packaged teas, but one or two gardens now market single-source self-drinkers.

Gunung Rosa

Characteristics
Large-leafed tea that gives an excellent, bright, light infusion with a hint of sweetness, not unlike some high-grown Ceylon teas.

Brewing hints
Brew 1 teaspoon in a scant 1 cup water at 203°F. Infuse for 3–4 minutes.

Drinking recommendations

Drink with or without milk, or perhaps with lemon. Excellent at tea time.

Taloon

Characteristics
Beautiful whole-leaf tea from Java with a lot of golden tips that gives a flavorful, aromatic infusion.

Brewing hints
Brew 1 teaspoon in a scant 1 cup water at 203°F. Infuse for 3–4 minutes.

Drinking recommendations

A good tea-time tea to drink with traditional afternoon tea foods.

Bah Butong

Characteristics
A broken leaf tea from Sumatra that gives a strong infusion with body and color.

Brewing hints
Brew 1 teaspoon in a scant cup water at 203°F. Infuse for 3–4 minutes.

Drinking recommendations

A breakfast tea.
Drink with milk.

JAPAN

Smooth waves of green tea bushes undulating over the landscape.

APANESE HISTORY SAYS THAT THE FIRST TEA SEEDS, brought from China by the Buddhist monk Dengyo Daishi, were planted in A.D. 805. It is also thought that some seeds were sent to the Abbot of Toga-no-o in Yamashiro, and some of the plants that grew were transplanted to Uji where the soil is particularly good. Tea from Uji is still thought to be the finest in the country. In about the same period, five major plantations were also laid out at Asahi, Kambayashi, Kyogoku, Yamana, and Umoji, and these are all still in existence today.

SOUTH KOREA

HONSHU

SAITAMA

KYOTO AICHI Mt Fuji **TOKYO**
SHIZUOKA
MIE
NARA

FUKUOKA
SAGA
KAGOSHIMA SHIKOKU

KYUSHU PACIFIC OCEAN

Mechanical plucking in a Japanese tea field.

Japanese tea gardens look quite different from plantations in other parts of the world. The bushes are cultivated side by side in long strips rather than spaced apart, giving the impression of smooth waves of green undulating over the landscape. The upper surface is curved and it is from these long regular plucking tables that the pickers take the buds and leaves.

After the Second World War, tea cultivation expanded, and the main areas of production are now the prefectures of Shizuoka, Kagoshima, Mie, Nara, Kyoto (around Uji), Saga, Fukuoka, and Saitama. Nishio in Aichi prefecture is famous for powdered teas.

The climate is warm with plenty of rain and the plantations are mostly located on the hills and close to rivers, streams, and lakes where the warmth combines with dense fogs and heavy dews. About 600,000 farming families produce approximately 110,231 tons of tea from 148,263 acres of land. The harvesting begins at the end of April and, after the leaves have been plucked by hand or by automatic scissors rather like electric hair clippers, they are transported to the factories where they go through various stages of processing, depending on the type of tea. All Japanese teas are green.

GREEN TEA VARIETIES

Gyokuro is the very best of Japan's teas. To produce high quality Gyokuro tea, the bushes must be kept under 90 percent shade from the beginning of May for about 20 days. As soon as the new buds begin to form, the entire plantation, or area of the plantation given over to the production of Gyokuro, is covered with mats of bamboo, reed, or canvas. The reduced light means that the tiny leaves develop a higher chlorophyll content (making the leaves a darker green than normal) and a lower tannin content (giving the tea a sweeter, milder flavor). When harvesting begins, only the softest freshest leaves are carefully plucked either by hand or automatic scissors rather like electric hair clippers. The leaves are then rushed to the factory and are steamed for about 30

seconds to seal in the flavor and arrest fermentation. Next, they are fluffed with hot air and then pressed and dried until only 30 percent of their original water content remains. Repeated rolling shapes the leaves into fine dark green needles. These are then sorted to remove any stalks and old leaves, and are then dried again.

To produce Tencha, a finely chopped tea that is ground when required to make Matcha (powdered tea) the bushes are also grown under 90 percent shade. Larger leaves than are picked for Gyokuro are gathered, steamed, and fluffed in the same way. They are dried without rolling so that they keep their original shape and are then cut into very small pieces. Because powdered green tea keeps for only a short time (four weeks in winter, two weeks in summer), the leaves are stored as Tencha, which keeps well, until powdered tea, Matcha, is required. Matcha is the tea that is drunk during the traditional Japanese Tea Ceremony. Finely chopped Tencha is ground to a fine powder using a stone mill. Both Gyokuro and Tencha tea are only harvested once a year because the shading drains the bushes of energy and they need time to recover.

Sencha is Japan's most popular everyday tea. Various qualities are manufactured—the best being served only on special occasions, and average quality brewed for everyday use at home and work. The bushes are grown in

Tea bushes are shaded so that the leaves develop a good flavor.

full sunlight and the first crop is harvested from late April to the middle of May. Most of the plucking is carried out with mechanical harvesting scissors or plucking machines, but the finest quality Sencha is plucked by hand. In some places, the leaves are gathered every 45 days, four times a year, and the first and second crops give the best leaf. The first crop gives a soft mild taste, while the second has a stronger flavor and contains more tannin and caffeine because of the strong sunlight in which the leaves develop. The leaves are processed in a

similar way as for Gyokuro and Tencha. They are first steamed, fluffed with hot air, then dried and rolled into fine needles.

Bancha is the lowest grade of Sencha tea. The larger, coarser, more fibrous leaves are gathered after the younger, more tender leaves that are used to make Sencha have been plucked from each new flush, and more are picked during the summer months. The processing is the same as for Sencha, but uses stems and stalks as well as leaves. When Bancha is roasted, it is called Houjicha. The roasting takes place after the usual steaming, fluffing, drying, and rolling, and the leaves are then finished to a wedge shape. Genmaicha is a mixture of Bancha with popped rice that has been boiled and dried.

Two other, more unusual, green teas are also made in Japan. Kanmairicha-Tamayokucha is produced using the old Chinese method of roasting the leaves in a pan to prevent oxidation and then drying and rolling them by hand to form little balls. Mecha is made from young leaves that are selected during the refining process of Gyokuro and Sencha and these are rolled to pin-head sized balls which give a strong liquor when infused.

Gyokuro (Precious Dew)

This is the very best of Japan's teas, and is always the one chosen to serve to visitors. Depending on quality, the water temperature and length of infusion should be adjusted accordingly.

Characteristics

This is the finest of Japan's teas. Leaves are beautiful, flat, pointed, emerald needles that give a smooth taste and a subtle perfume. This is a very refined and special tea.

Brewing hints

For three people, brew 4 teaspoons in 4 tablespoons previously boiled water at 122–140°F. Steep for 1½–2 minutes. Add more water for further infusions.

Drinking recommendations

Drink on very special occasions after a meal, or as an uplifting, cleansing, and refreshing drink at any time.

Matcha Uji (Froth of Liquid Jade)

The whisking of this powder into hot water helps to dissolve the tea and produces a froth that is thought to enhance the flavor.

Characteristics

High quality Matcha manufactured in the Uji region. Powdered tea from leaf grown under 90 percent shade gives a rich, astringent jade liquor.

Brewing hints

Place a generous ½ teaspoon into a deep bowl, add 8 teaspoons previously boiled water at 185°F, and whisk with a bamboo whisk for 30 seconds.

Drinking recommendations

This is a nourishing beverage suitable for all times of the day.

Sencha

Sencha is available in a wide variety of qualities and prices. This average quality Sencha is intended for everyday use and is commonly found in homes and offices.

Characteristics
Large-leafed everyday Sencha. Clear sparkling liquor with the typical delicate Japanese flavor. Rich in vitamin C.

Brewing hints
For five people, brew 4 teaspoons in 1¾ cups previously boiled water at 194°F. Infuse for 1–1½ minutes. Warm the tea cups or bowls with boiling water before serving.

Drinking recommendations

Drink with meals or as a digestif.

Also recommended
Sencha Honyama, Sencha Sayama, and Sencha Yame.

Bancha

Bancha means "late harvest" and is made from large hard leaves including the stems and red stalks. Because the flavor is weaker, it is suitable for children and invalids.

Characteristics
The coarser leaf contains less caffeine and tannin, and gives a weaker, less interesting infusion.

Brewing hints
For five people, brew 6 teaspoons in 2⅔ cups water at 203–212°F. Infuse for 30 seconds.

Drinking recommendations

Drink with meals or as a cold refreshing drink in summer.

Houjicha

Houjicha was invented in 1920 by a merchant in Kyoto who did not know what to do with a surplus stock of old leaves until he had the idea of roasting them and so created a tea with a new flavor.

Characteristics
Light brown roasted leaves give a light brown liquor. Very gentle on the stomach.

Brewing hints
For five people, brew 6 teaspoons in 2⅔ cups water at 203–212°F. Infuse for 30 seconds.

Drinking recommendations

Drink with food or as a comforting bedtime drink.

Genmaicha

Hulled rice kernels and popped corn add an interesting flavor to Bancha.

Characteristics
Medium quality tea that gives a light brown refreshing infusion with a slightly savory flavor.

Brewing hints
For one person, brew 1¼ teaspoons in a scant 1 cup water at 203°F. Infuse for 1 minute.

Drinking recommendations

An all-day tea, especially good with light foods.

Other recommended Japanese teas
Fuji Yama, Kukicha, Ureshinocha, and Kawanecha.

TAIWAN

Home of Tung Ting, the best of Formosa teas.

THE FIRST TEA BUSHES WERE PLANTED in Formosa (as it then was) 300 years ago. Plants were taken from China's Fujian Province and planted in the north of the country. Today, most of the tea comes from this region around T'ai-pei. The plantations are all below 1,000 feet, where the temperatures never fall below 55°F or rise above 82°F. The bushes flush five times a year from April to December, and the best leaf is picked between the end of May and mid-August. Nearly all Formosa teas are oolongs, with occasional lightly fermented pouchongs also being manufactured. Most of these latter teas are used as a base for Jasmine and other scented teas.

In the past, Japan was the major buyer of Formosa teas, but in recent years, Morocco and the U.S. have started importing larger quantities.

Formosa Gunpowder

Characteristics

Little, round green tea pellets that give a deliciously clean, refreshing infusion.

Brewing hints

Brew 2 teaspoons in a scant 1 cup water at 203°F. Infuse for 3 minutes.

Drinking recommendations

Excellent alone or flavored with mint. A wonderful afternoon tea.

Formosa Grand Pouchong

Characteristics

Very lightly fermented, almost green tea. This is a competitor to Tung Ting, Taiwan's famous tea. Pale yellow-golden infusion and delicate aroma.

Brewing hints

Brew 1 teaspoon in a scant 1 cup water at 203°F. Infuse for 4–5 minutes.

Drinking recommendations

Drink all day or as a soothing evening tea.

Formosa Great Oolong (Great Black Dragon)

Characteristics

For this exceptional tea, the white-tipped leaves are picked during the spring. Beautiful whole leaf, delicate flavor, and exquisite aroma.

Brewing hints

Brew 1 teaspoon in a scant 1 cup water at 203°F. Infuse for 7 minutes.

Drinking recommendations

Drink without milk. Save for very special occasions.

Tung Ting

Characteristics

Considered to be Taiwan's best tea. It is a lightly fermented Pouchong that gives an orangy-green liquor with a gentle, smooth light taste.

Brewing hints

Brew 1 teaspoon in a scant 1 cup water at 203°F. Infuse for 5–7 minutes.

Drinking recommendations

✪

Drink without milk on very special occasions.

Other recommended Formosa teas Grand Pouchong Imperial, Oolong Imperial, and Ti Kwan Yin.

OTHER

TEA-

PRODUCING

COUNTRIES

SOUTH AMERICA

ARGENTINA

Argentina produces 95 percent of its tea in in the province of Misiones, and the remaining 5 percent in Corrientes. Because of an acute shortage of labor, mechanical plucking methods are now used. This has improved plucking productivity by 2,000 percent. Argentina's teas give a dark liquor with an earthy taste and medium body. Most are exported to China and the U.S. for blending or for the production of instant tea.

Recommended garden
Misiones.

Mechanical harvesting machines with pneumatic elevator and bulk bin.

177

BRAZIL

Brazil produces orthodox black tea that is grown in the area south of São Paulo. Most is used for tea bag blends for the U.K. and the domestic market. The teas are generally of better quality than those produced in Argentina, and give clear, bright liquors but flavor is lacking. Best drunk with milk.

Recommended garden
São Paulo.

ECUADOR

This country has been growing tea since the late 1960s and much of the black tea that is produced is exported to the U.S. for blending. The teas tend to give quite strong liquors with good flavor, although sometimes they are a little earthy.

PERU

Tea is grown in the two departments of Cusco and Huanuco and production is approximately 1,874 tons a year. There have been plans in the past year or two to use 500 tons of their total yearly production to make instant tea since there is a large demand for it in the domestic market, but due to economic problems, this idea has had to be put on hold for the moment.

AFRICA

BURUNDI

Burundi started commercial production of tea in the early 1970s and in 1994 produced 7,566.3 tons from 22,400 acres of land. There are five tea-producing factories, four of which are situated at above 6,000 feet. Like Rwanda, the country has suffered over the past few years from civil strife and political instability, and this has affected tea production and quality. With hilly terrain and a tropical climate, the area has great potential for excellent quality teas of a similar type to Rwanda and could produce some very useful and interesting teas in the coming years.

Recommended garden
Teza-Ijenda.

Tea picking in Burundi.

ETHIOPIA

Ethiopia has two tea-producing factories in the south of the country on a plateau near

Gumaro tea plantation has 2,125 acres under tea.

the Kenyan border. About 4,942 acres of bushes grow at elevations above 5,500 feet and produce teas similar to those of Kenya. The tea industry has good potential for an improvement in quality and increased production now that the country is politically more stable.

MADAGASCAR

The island's clonal teas are grown at 5,500 feet and the manufactured black leaf gives bright colory teas with an attractive quality similar to the best of East African teas. Production is seasonal, with dry weather prevailing from May to September when very little tea is produced.

Recommended garden
Sahambavy.

MAURITIUS

Tea, the beverage, was introduced to Mauritius by the Frenchman Pierre Poivre in 1770. The island today produces some reasonable teas that have strength and color but are not of particularly good quality. The country is beginning to pull out of tea production in favor of sugar and textiles, because of a drop in world tea prices, and by the year 2001, will probably stop tea production altogether.

M O Z A M B I Q U E

The Portuguese planted tea in the Zambesi province of Mozambique but in recent years, because of the political unrest in the 1970s, production has declined. The strong black teas have a lightly spiced taste and are good as breakfast teas, drunk with milk.

R W A N D A

The tea industry was established in Rwanda in the 1950s with financial assistance from the Belgian government and the E.C. With fertile soil, a beneficial pattern of rainfall, and a very suitable climate, the tea flourished, managing to produce consistent quality similar to that of the best of Africa's CTC teas. However, the beginning of political problems in 1990 meant severe disruption in production.

The largest factory at Mulindi was occupied by invading Batutsies and, in 1994, all the factories ceased production. It was thought unlikely, during the civil war, that any part of the industry could function for quite some time, but in September 1994, the estate of Cyohoha Rukeri started production again, after major pruning of the neglected bushes, and the factory was back in action in February 1995. Production in 1995 was more than 2,204.6 tons and quality has been brought back to pre-war levels. With the refurbishment of factories and the rehabilitation of plantations, quality and quantity are expected to return quickly to previous standards.

Recommended gardens
Kitabi and Matah.

U G A N D A

Tea cultivation in Uganda started in 1909 but there was little commercial development until the late 1920s when private plantations were established by former First World War soldiers. From the mid 1950s, there was rapid expansion in production on estates that were almost all owned by white planters. Until 1972, both the private commercial estates and smallholdings expanded so that Uganda had 47,160 acres of tea, and tea became the country's most important export. But, the political instability of the 1970s and 1980s badly affected the industry, and tea exports dropped from 26,455.5 tons in 1972 to 1,102.3 tons in 1980.

Tea plantations were damaged or abandoned, factories ran at reduced capacity or, closed down, because of lack of electricity, spare parts, or labor—or all three. Since 1989, political stability has returned and with it there has been major rehabilitation of plantations and factories, and production has risen steadily. From a total production of 5.1 tons of tea in 1989, the figure for 1994 had reached 16.3 tons.

However, problems do still exist. Exchange rates have not helped Uganda's industry, transport costs are high, there is a lack of skilled and unskilled labor, power supplies are unpredictable and unreliable, factories are old and need further refurbishment, and since 1988, there has been no funding for research activities.

Mechanically harvested tea bushes in Uganda.

Prices for Ugandan teas at the Mombasa and London auctions have been low over recent years, because of a lack of consistency of quality. But as production expands and improves, prices are slowly increasing and there are hopes that production will soon reach 1972 levels of 26,455.5 tons by 1998, and possibly double by the year 2000.

Recommended garden
Mityana.

ZIMBABWE

Zimbabwe has two main tea-growing regions, Chipinge and Honde Valley. Teas are of a similar type to those produced in Malawi, and give a strong dark-colored brew. Most are exported to the U.K. for blending as tea bag tea. Some clonal tea is also now being produced. Best with milk.

Recommended garden
Southbown.

EUROPE

THE AZORES

THE AZORES

Tea is grown on the island of San Miguel which was formed as the result of a volcanic eruption. Tea was brought to the island from Brazil in the 1820s and by the first half of the twentieth century there were about 741 acres of land under tea. However, by 1966,

this had decreased to approximately 380 acres, and, due to a lack of technical understanding of tea cultivation, the quality of the tea was very poor.

In 1984 the Azores government brought in a tea expert from Mozambique, and a program is now underway to recuperate the old plantations, introduce new plants, mechanize pruning and plucking, improve cultivation processes, and generally improve quality. The operation is very small and most of the teas produced are sold to the tourists who visit the island. In 1995 the government granted money to be spent on the cultivation and manufacture of tea and there are hopes of increasing both quality and production with a view to supplying the local market and exporting to the U.S. and elsewhere.

ASIA

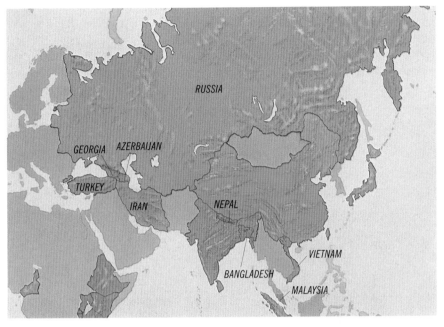

RUSSIA

GEORGIA AZERBAIJAN

TURKEY

IRAN NEPAL

VIETNAM

BANGLADESH

MALAYSIA

BANGLADESH

After the British had established tea production in Assam in the 1830s, cultivation quickly expanded into Sylhet and what were then other north Indian areas. After partition in 1947, and later separation for West Pakistan when East Pakistan was renamed Bangladesh, the tea-growing areas of Sylhet and around Chittagong continued to be very important.

Harvesting goes on from April to December and the best teas are gathered in May and June. The majority of production is of black tea, some of which is packed as leaf grades at individual factories, with most of the dust, fannings, and smaller broken grades going for blending, and a smaller weight of green tea. Annual production is approximately 56,217.9 tons, of which about 36,376.3 tons are exported. Major foreign buyers are Pakistan and Poland, with smaller amounts going to the U.K., C.I.S. countries, Russia, Germany, Egypt, China, Iran, Australia, New Zealand, Sudan, Belgium, and India. The teas are similar in character to south Indian teas, giving good color and aroma and a slightly spicy flavor. They are best drunk with milk.

Recommended garden
Chittagong.

C . I . S .

AZERBAIJAN

Azerbaijan's main areas of production are Lenkoran, Masallin, Lerik, and Astar. Total production in 1988 was 38,580 tons, but this dropped to 9,369 tons in 1992 and was as low as 1,213 tons by 1995. Since then

however, output has begun to increase and two joint ventures have been established with Turkey and the United Arab Emirates.

GEORGIA

Before the civil war of 1993-1995, Georgia's main growing areas were West Georgia and Abkhazia Province. Since 1993, production has almost ceased.

RUSSIA

Cultivation in Russia goes back to 1833 when tea seeds were planted in the Nikity Botanical Gardens in the Crimea. However, the industry did not develop until after the

Tea plantation at Sochi in Krasnodar Province, Russia.

First World War and expanded rapidly after the Second World War. Russia's main producing region today is Krasnodar Province in the south west of the country.

Before the disintegration of the USSR, the total area under tea was 3,707 acres with an annual production of 3,858-4,409 tons from two factories. By the mid 1990s, production had almost been totally discontinued.

IRAN

Since 1900, Iran has been growing tea in the north of the country. The black leaf gives a reddish, light, smooth liquor. The teas are best drunk without milk.

Recommended garden
Elbourz.

MALAYSIA

The Cameron Highlands plantation, not far from Kuala Lumpur, was laid out in 1929 by the son of a British government official. He called it Boh after Bohea, the district in China where, according to legend, tea was first discovered. Original labor came from India but, although some of the original staff still work on the plantation, new workers now come from Bangladesh.

Boh plantation produces 70 percent of Malaysia's tea in what are near perfect climatic conditions. The teas are fair quality orthodox black teas with quite light, bright liquors rather like those of medium quality Ceylon teas.

Recommended gardens
Boh and Blue Valley.

A variety of teas from Malaysia.

NEPAL

The Nepalese government has encouraged tea cultivation on the slopes of the Himalayas, and the black leaf produced gives a smooth, subtle, perfumed brew. Export is very limited because of high local demand.

TURKEY

Turkey's plantations, which have been in operation since 1938, are in the Rize region close to the Black Sea and produce 110,231 tons per year. The factories produce medium grade black teas, the bulk of which are consumed locally and very little is exported. The small leafed tea gives a dark liquor but the flavor is gentle and almost sweet, rather like Russia's teas. Best drunk with milk.

VIETNAM

The French established the first tea plantations in 1825, but the industry suffered badly from the continuous conflict in the area. Tea was not given priority in the rehabilitation of the country after the war but, in tea terms, Vietnam is a sleeping giant. There is still a lot of tea in the ground and companies are now looking at the viability of rehabilitation. Decentralization has enabled individual provinces to deal directly with foreign companies, and licences have been granted to companies with a proven track record over a number of years. The estates currently produce about 44,092.4 tons of tea annually, of which 27,557.8 tons are green teas, Black teas are CTC and are mostly exported to Germany.

OCEANIA

AUSTRALIA

The Australian tea industry produces only 1,653.5 tons of tea per year, mostly black tea and a small amount of green tea. The first estate was laid out in Queensland in the late 1880s, but this was wiped out by a cyclone in 1918. The industry was re-established in 1959 with the planting of the Nerada plantation near Innisfail, and plantations on Mount Bartle Frere in Queensland, and in Clothiers Creek in the northern part of New

A variety of teas available from Madura Tea Estates.

South Wales. The black teas are mainly CTC for tea bag blends, some leaf tea for packages, and orthodox green teas that have a twisted appearance like that of the green teas produced by many Asian countries.

Recommended gardens
Nerada and Madura.

PAPUA NEW GUINEA

Conditions of both climate and soil in Papua New Guinea are excellent for tea. Forested and mountainous inland, with swampy plains toward the coast. Cultivation is in the Western Highlands and most of the black teas produced are sold to Australia.

ADDRESSES

MAIL-ORDER TEA COMPANIES

U.K.

Betty's & Taylors of Harrogate
1 Parliament Street
Harrogate
HG1 2QU
Tel: (44-1423) 886055

The Tea and Coffee Trading Company
6/7 Market Place
Hitchin
Hertfordshire
SG5 1DR
Tel: (44-1462) 433631

St. James's Teas Ltd.
Sir John Lyon House
5 Upper Thames Street
London
EC4V 3PA
Tel: (44-171) 2360611
Fax: (44-171) 4540006

Whittard of Chelsea
73 Northcote Road
London
SW11 6PJ
Tel: (44-171) 9241888
Fax: (44-171) 9243085

U.S.

Choice Organic Teas
Granum Inc.
2901 NE. Blakely Street
Seattle, WA 98105
Tel: (1-206) 525 0051
Fax: (1-206) 523 9750

Grace Tea Company Ltd.
50 West 17th Street
New York, NY 10011
Tel/Fax: (1-212) 255 2935

Harney & Sons Ltd.
Village Green
P.O. Box 638
Salisbury, CT 06068
Tel: (1-203) 435 9218
Fax: (1-203) 435 2724

Imperial Tea Court
1411 Powell Street
San Francisco, CA 94133
Tel: (1-415) 788 6080
Fax: (1-415) 788 6079

Mark T. Wendell, Importer
P.O. Box 946
Pasadena, CA 91102
Tel/Fax: 1—800 946 3329

O'Mona Tea International
9 Pine Ridge Road
Ryebrook, NY 10573
Tel: (1-914) 937 8858

Simpson & Vail
P.O. Box 309
Pleasantville, NY 10570
Tel: 1—800 282 8327
Fax: (1-914) 741 6942

The Stash Tea Company
P.O. Box 910
Portland, Oregon 97207
Tel: (1-503) 684 4482
Fax: (1-503) 624 9744

Ten Ren Tea
75 Mott Street
New York, NY 10013
Tel: 1—800 292 2049
Fax: (1-212) 349 2180

Upton Tea Imports
231 South Street
Hopkinton, MA 01748
Tel: (1-508) 435 9988
Fax: (1-508) 435 9955

CANADA

Murchie's Tea and Coffee Ltd
5580 Parkwood Way
Richmond
British Columbia
Canada V6V2M4
Tel: (1-604) 231 7422
Fax: (1-604) 231 7466

AUSTRALIA

Madura Tea Estates
Clothiers Creek Road
Clothiers Creek
New South Wales 2484
Tel: (61-66) 777215
Fax: (61-66) 777451

FRANCE

Mariage Frères
30 rue de Bourg-Tibourg
Le Marais
75004 Paris
Tel: (33-1) 42 72 28 11

TEA MAGAZINES

Tea—A Magazine
Olde English Tea Company Inc.
3 Devotion Road
P.O. Box 348
Scotland,
CT 06264
U.S.A.
Tel: (1-203) 456 6145
Fax: (1-203) 456 1023

**Tea and Coffee Trade
Journal** (incorporating Tea
International)
Lockwood Publishing
130 West 42nd Street
10th Floor
New York,
NY 10036
U.S.A.

Tea Talk
P.O. Box 860
Sausalito, CA 94966
Tel/Fax: (1-415) 331 1557

Mary Mac's Tea Times
P.O. Box 841
Langley, WA 98260
U.S.A.

OTHER USEFUL ADDRESSES

**The Bramah Tea and
Coffee Museum**
The Clove Building
4 Maguire Street
London SE1 2NQ
U.K.
Tel: (44-171) 3780222
Fax: (44-171) 3780219

Twinings
The Golden Lion
216 Strand
London WC2R 1AP
U.K.

The U.K. Tea Council
Sir John Lyon House
5 Upper Thames Street
London EC4 3NJ
Tel: (44-171) 2481024
Fax: (44-171) 3294568

The U.S. Tea Council
230 Park Avenue
New York City, NY 10169
Tel: (1-212) 986 6998
Fax: (1-212) 697 8658

INDEX

ACKNOWLEDGMENTS

The Publisher would like to thank the following individuals, companies,
and organizations for their contribution to this publication:
Mr Edward Bramah, at the Bramah Tea and Coffee Museum, for allowing his collection
to be photographed; Bodum (UK) Ltd. for the loan of the teawares featured on pg 50 (b) and pg 51;
Whittards of Chelsea for loaning the spring-handled infuser (pg 52), infuser mugs (pg 53b), and swivel
tea strainer (pg 58); Simpson & Vail, Inc. for supplying the mesh teaball, muslin infuser, mesh pot
infuser, infuser spoon (pg 52), bamboo strainer and English tea strainer (pg 58); Stash Tea for supplying
the teaball infuser and Swiss gold tea filter (pg 52); Su Russell at College Farm Tea House, Finchley,
London for kindly allowing us to photograph the afternoon tea shot on her premises, featured on pg 87.

All teas featured in the Directory were supplied by Mariage Frères, Paris, except for: Gunung Rosa –
Matthew Algie & Company Limited; Pouchong, Keemun Mao Feng, Gyokuro – India Tea Importers; Ndu,
Djuttitsu Clonal, Tole, Namingomba, Kavuzi, Kilima – Wilson Smithett; Zulu Tea – Taylors of Harrogate;
Houjicha, Bancha, Jasmine Pearl – Whittards of Chelsea; Sencha, Genmaicha – Simpson & Vail, Inc.;
Assam Blend, Darjeeling Blend, Rose Pouchong, Kenya Blend – Twinings.

PICTURE CREDITS